TRUE LIFE IN GOD

Vassula: Conversation with Jesus

Published and Distributed by:-

J.M.J. Publications
P.O. Box 385
Belfast BT9 6RQ
Northern Ireland
Fax: (0232) 381596

His Holiness Pope Paul VI has confirmed on
October 14, 1966, the decree of the Sacred
Congregation for the propagation of the Faith,
under number 58/16 (A.A.S.), permitting the
publication of writings about supernatural
apparitions, even if they do not have a "nihil
obstat" from ecclesiastical authorities.

TABLE OF CONTENTS
NOTEBOOKS 59-64

TREASURES OF MY SACRED HEART

April 9th, 1992 - Arizona

Lord?

I Am. I give you My Peace; bless Me.

I bless You my King.

If anyone asks you for a message from Me tell them that I have already poured out My Heart on them, therefore I have spoken to them through you.[1] I have poured on them the <u>Treasures of My Sacred Heart</u> - this <u>is</u> <u>My</u> Message for all of them.
ΙΧΘΥΣ ⊂▷

BEAR FRUIT IN HOLINESS

April 10th, 1992 - Arizona

At the Church of Our Lady of Perpetual Help.

Tell My children: bear fruit in holiness. I have offered you My Heart - what will you do with It?

Vassula, remember My Presence: My Presence is Joy, Peace, Love and Holiness.
♥

---

[1]That is: through this whole revelation.

BE OBEDIENT TO LOVES DESIRE SO THAT EVERYONE SEES THAT YOU ARE MY DISCIPLE

April 17th, 1992

So long as Your Breath blows on me
You will keep renewing me
and on my feet.
Breathe on me, so that I may not die Lord.
Invade my soul with Your Light.
Yahweh my God
clothed in impressive Glory
may You be blessed.

Amen.

Be in Peace. Allow Me to lead you as I please. I love you eternally. Never doubt of My Love. Come My child, together you and I, together in union with Me. Together bonded to My Cross, we will bring many souls back to Me; do your best and I shall do the rest; let Me use you for My Glory till the end. Delight My Sacred Heart and remain nothing; let your heart be My Heaven. I shall continue providing your soul. Praise Me often and love Me, love this Heart of your Lord; love this lacerated Heart of your Master. Desire Me and thirst for Me your King. Despise yourself so that you remain in My Love and will not be deceived; do not look to your left nor to your right, I shall then perform even greater works through you. You are pruned now and then but I noticed how your weak nature dislikes it! Everything I do is done with wisdom from Wisdom Herself, so My Vassula, allow Me to prune you now and then; believe Me, it is necessary for your growth. I have chosen you for this mission to go out to the nations and to bear fruit. I know how frail you are and how much Satan would like to see you annihilated from the surface of the earth but I am by your side. Therefore, never complain but accept all of your trials graciously with love and with great humility; the devil will be disarmed and will flee with these virtues. Never give the devil a foothold.
♥

No one yet has grasped the breadth and the length the height and the depth of My Love. I want you entirely for Me, just for Me - I am telling you this over and over again from the very beginning when I called you. I have espoused you to Me for My glorification so that you work together with Me. Your mind now should be set on Me and Me alone. Pray all the time asking Me for all the things you need. Be obedient to Love's desires so that everyone sees that you are My disciple; I took you to Myself to make you live a holy life under My Light. Remember: you have one

Master and that is Me; you have one Father and that is Me; you have one Spouse and that is Me; you have one Love and that is Me. I have taught you to live by the Truth and in Love to enable you to grow in Me. Once you were ignorant of Me and enslaved to the world and to creatures, but I, your Creator, have detached you so that you love Me above everything and above all. Today I am asking you: are you happy to be with Me in this way?

I am very happy Lord, You know it.

You have become an object of dread for Satan, this is why you see now and feel his fury. The more your fruit increased, the more fires he built, accumulating falsehood and fraud to accuse you. He wrestles with the angel I have given you; he amasses fraud against you yet, in spite of all this, do you still want to continue this Divine Work with Me?

I, your slave out of love, shall serve Your Greatness and Your Majesty till the end.

♥ *My beloved one, I will continue then to lead you with reins of love.* ♥ *Come.*

MY WORDS ON YOU ARE ALIVE AND ARE SPIRIT

April 18th, 1992

Fraud and oppression fill their mouth, spite and iniquity are under their tongue; there in the reeds they lie in ambush to kill the innocent where no one can see. Psalm 10:7-8 (Samek) Pe.

My poor and wretched instrument, grow in My Love. I am He who adopts you, so be in My Love and grow in My Love; you will eat out of My Riches to reveal Me and glorify Me. Blessed of My Soul write:

Where there is mistrust and rational thinking there is also arguing and contention; this sort of people intellectually are living in darkness and are estranged from the Spirit's Works. Daughter, they have not yet perceived My Beauty... I have chosen your heart, My child, to become My Tablet upon which I would write My Love Song to all My children; I made out of you a Hymn of Love. My words are not printed only, My words on you are alive and are Spirit. I have given you sound teaching. Do not worry about those who come to you with unending arguments and with a craze for questioning everything and arguing about words; these people are the prey to the Tempter and are allowing the Tempter, by giving him a foothold, to get trapped into ambitions. Lay your hands upon these people and bless them: "in the Name of the Father, and of the Son and of the Holy Spirit." You will honour Me and glorify Me. IXθYΣ ✕◁▷

TREAT YOUR NATURAL DESIRES OF THE FLESH HARD THE WORLD HAS EXCHANGED MY DIVINITY FOR A WORTHLESS IMITATION

April 19th, 1992

Cities are raised on a single Blessing from Your Mouth, altars in ruin are rebuilt by an instant look from You and the dead come to life with a single breath from You to extol Your Holy Name, and all those whom You covered with Your radiant dew made their peace with You, but everything is demolished by the mouth of the wicked. Death does not extol You, it is the living who praise You day and night.

You have said well, daughter. The prize of the victory is with all of you[1], double your prayers, your sacrifices and your fasting; treat your natural desires of the flesh hard; treat your body hard and do not allow it to comply with its cravings, make your body obey you. Be in a constant prayer to Me and in every course you take have Me in mind. I am your God. Pray for your brothers and sisters who follow a false religion,[2] a false image of Myself. The devil has gone down to your generation in a rage, these sects were prophesied in the Scripture. Vassula, these false religions have spread in My Church[3] like cancer in a body; these sects are the cancer of My Body. They may argue that true wisdom is to be found in them but Satan is trying to deceive if possible all the world, even the elect. The world's stubborn refusal to repent has led it to error; your generation knew Me, yet it refused to recognize Me. It preferred to follow in its obscured mind Satan's doctrines. I have offered My Peace but the world refused My Peace; the world instead exchanged My Glory for a Lie; it exchanged My Perpetual Sacrifice for the disastrous abomination:

the spirit of rebellion

---

[1] That is: Victory depends from us.
[2] Sects like Jehovah Witnesses, New Age, Moonies etc...
[3] We are all the Lord's Church.

given by the Rebel. *The world has exchanged My Divinity for a worthless imitation: a mortal man. It has given up Divine Truth for a Lie; but, it has been said[1] that at the end of Time, Satan will set to work and that there will be all kinds of miracles and a great deal of a deceptive show of signs[2] and portents and everything evil that can deceive those who are bound for destruction because they would not grasp the Love of the Truth which could have saved them, this is the reason why I am sending a power to delude them and make them believe what is untrue is to condemn all who refused to believe in the truth and chose wickedness instead. The power of the Rebel[3] is such that he has without any fear appeared openly now to everyone, this is the one of which the prophet Ezekiel[4] spoke of, the one swollen with pride, the one who claims to be God, <u>the one who apes the Truth</u>, the one who considers himself as My equal and says that he sits on My Throne. The Rebel is indeed the Enemy of My Church, the Antichrist, the man who denies the Holy Trinity. Have you not read: "the man who denies that Jesus is the Christ, he is a liar, he is Antichrist and he is denying the Father as well as the Son because no one who has the Father can deny the Son, and to acknowledge the Son is to have the Father as well."[5] These doctrines of Satan teach you to believe in reincarnation, whereas there is <u>no</u> reincarnation; they keep up the outward appearance of religion but have rejected the inner power of it - the Holy Spirit and the Holy Communion, My child. Satan goes disguised as an angel of light to deceive many, and together with the Rebel[6] he will confer great honours on those who will acknowledge him, by giving them wide authority and by farming out the land at a price[7]; but I tell you truly, that soon heaven will open and My Fire will come down on them and consume them.*

Faithful and True, I Am.
Judge and Integrity
I Am.
The Word of God
I Am.
The King of kings and the Lord of lords
I Am.

---

[1] 2 Thessalonians 2:9-12.
[2] Satan, aping God, can give even the stigmatas, like he has given them to someone belonging to the sect of New Age.
[3] Freemasonry.
[4] Ezekiel 28:1.
[5] 1 John: 2:22-23.
[6] Daniel 11:39.
[7] Freemasons.

6

and I repeat to you My Promise:

I shall indeed be with you soon. ♥

OFFER ME EVERYTHING TO ASSUAGE MY THIRST

April 20th, 1992

Yahweh, I am Your slave and I will offer You again today my will that You may do what Your Heart pleases with me. What a delight to be in Your Presence and to be allowed to walk with Your Majesty! What return can I make to You for all the blessings You poured on me? I have only to lift my eyes towards Heaven and You bend down to listen to me; and when I invoke Your Name, Your Majesty descends all the way from Your Throne, You who are Sovereign in the Heavens and on earth to be with me in my room and keep me company.

I come to you. Misery attracts Me, poverty infatuates Me; so do not weary yourself with getting rich. Set Me, your God, like a seal on your heart and I shall continue, My beloved one, to demonstrate My sweetness towards you.

My God is good to me, a stronghold when I am oppressed and calumniated, a stronghold when times are hard. My God is my protective Shield. Satan may sharpen his sword or may bend his bow and take aim on me, but my God, my Abba ever so Tender, will be present and will make the devil flee.

Give Me unbounded love, I am looking down from Heaven at you all to see if a single one is seeking Me without self-interest. What joy and what happiness I receive every time I hear My Name extolled! but many have turned aside, many are tainted with sin. Let My Heart rejoice in poverty; let My Heart rejoice in a love without self-interests. Give Me, daughter, as I have given you. Do not appear to Me empty-handed.

My gifts are Yours, in fact all the gifts I have been given <u>are</u> Yours.

Offer Me sacrifices, be generous, have I not been generous to you? Give Me now, as I have given you; offer Me sacrifices to appease My Justice[1]; build what I have given you to construct. ♥[2] *O Vassula! Offer Me everything to assuage My thirst! Put your faith in Me; <u>give</u> those who wait for My Word My Hymn of Love; <u>give</u> so that all the earth's inhabitants may hear My Merciful Cry.[3] I cannot ignore My children's supplication.*

Lord, I beg You to guide my steps in the Truth and in the Light.

You will continue then to minister before Me and I shall open your mouth to fill it with My Words to glorify Me ♥ *and through you I shall produce a visible Image of Myself. I will touch the hearts of My people and even people who never knew Me will be blessing Me. Despise yourself and I shall not reject you. I, Yahweh, will save you.*

WHAT COULD I HAVE DONE MORE THAT I HAVE NOT DONE? I HAVE INSCRIBED YOU IN THE FLESH OF MY HEART

April 20th, 1992

Come back to us and dwell in the middle of our heart. Let our heart be called: Faithful City and Your Holy Mountain.

Little one I give you My Peace. ♥ *The advices and the supplications from your Holy Mother,[4] My agonies and cries from My Holy Cross to the world have remained stagnant. We have come to offer you all Our Peace, and prepare you for your journey to heaven, but <u>Love has been rebuked and Peace treacherously replaced by lethargy and a spirit of wickedness.</u> I went in all directions seeking by what means I might awaken you from your perpetual lethargy and return to Me to live Holy, but I heard no sound from you. What could I have done more that I have not done? My friends, you have not taken seriously Our Calls; I descended*

---

[1] I hesitated. I did not know what did God exactly mean.
[2] I still did not understand.
[3] I finally understood that I have to continue more than ever to witness and make known God's Message.
[4] I understood, our Holy Mother of Medjugorje.

to offer you My Heart; I have inscribed you in the flesh of My Heart; I have written you My Love Hymn to all of you;

- I visited you -

My Eyes stream with Tears and Our Two Hearts are lacerated because you have not persevered in the Path of Holiness. The world made fun of Our Merciful Calls and no one was really listening. I am your God and Shield, full of Tenderness and I am known to intervene quickly in times of tribulations, but you preferred to walk in the shadows of darkness and in the valley of death. My kindness has been repaid with your wickedness arraigning Me for trying to save you... My Hymn of Love[1] to you is constantly being ridiculed, defamed and blasphemed for in your spirit lies a spirit of darkness. You are harvesting in the Deceiver's field to show the world that My Holy Words are ignominious with no substance,[2] but there too[3] you will be wasting your breath when you will come to Me for help in the days of purification; you will call, but I shall not listen. Men intent on silencing Me, laying snares; others are hatching treacherous plots all day long. The wicked may hope to destroy you, My child; you whom I have chosen, treating you like the scum of the earth, but I have sworn to maintain you on your feet - I shall uphold you for My purpose. I have told you, My child, that your persecutors will be allowed to give you impressive wounds, but they are for My Glory and for your purification. Your life-span is nothing and you are but a passing shadow on earth and your wounds and sufferings on earth are only a puff of wind compared to Mine. It is I, your Saviour who have kept your soul in My Arms and made your spirit live for Me alone; it is I, the Sublime Glory, that put in your mouth a New Hymn of Love to sing it to the world and melt its hardened heart. Look, you have given Me a drop or two of your life, and I, how much have I given you? I have given you to drink from the Eternal Fountains of My Breast, I never failed you. In an arduous battle I won your heart, puny little creature and made you Mine. I have treated you leniently and gently more than anyone else in spite of your childish insolence. I, your Creator, was charmed by your ineffable weakness and misery, and you, My creature, were left in awe by My perfect Beauty and My dazzling Light. You are clay and out of the same clay I modelled and shaped others too. ♥ I blew Life into you and made out of each one of you a portrait of My Image. I ask you to read: 'teach us to count how few days we have and so gain wisdom of heart.' (Psalm 90:12) Your passage on earth is as I said a passing shadow, so cling to Me, you do not have to prove your innocence.[4] I, your

---

[1] That is: The Messages of 'True Life in God.'
[2] Jesus is referring to these people who decided to twist every word in these Messages to prove to the world that these Messages are foul and not from God.
[3] Like in other times of persecution.
[4] My accusers have met between them to judge and condemn me as not from God. They even took all the trouble to write a book against me. (5 people)

Creator, know you. My child whom I have chosen, do not be afraid - come to Me and I shall warm you; do not be afraid when you are glorifying Me. Soon all that I foretold will take place and now when the former predictions will come true, many will shudder when they realize that:

**The Lamb sitting on the Throne
of God**

had truly sent among them a bearer, a bearer with good news and with a Hymn of Love in her mouth, to sing to all nations this New Hymn of the Most High, just as she had heard it from the Source of Sublime Love Himself, and that truly you were Mine from the beginning.

THOSE WHO SEEK ME EAGERLY SHALL FIND ME

April 23rd, 1992

My God, rationalism, modernism, the sects and atheism have invaded Your Glory. They have desecrated Your Holy Temple and defiled Your Sacred Name. They have reduced Your Sanctuary to a pile of ruins. They have left on their passage corpses of Your children, a prey for the vultures. How much longer will You be away, Lord? For long?

SHEPHERD!

Where are You? Apostasy is devouring Your sheep and rationalism is battering Your sheepfold. In tenderness quickly intervene, we can hardly be crushed lower; help us, God our Saviour, for the honour of Your Holy Name. We are Your people, are we not? The flock that You pasture.

Shepherd?

How much longer, Shepherd? Why hold back Your steps? O pick your steps over these endless ruins. Apostasy roared where Your Heart used to be, determined to destroy all that came out of Your Hand.

My Shepherd

loudly I cry to You, our strength is running out, so tell me, how much longer have we to wait? The time has come to have Mercy on us, hear our sighs, and let our cry reach You! Amen.

Soul! I, your Shepherd have leaned down from the heights of My Dwelling, have looked down at earth from heaven to hear the sighing of My lambs and to rescue those doomed to die savagely. As

My Word

has become a lamp to your feet a light on your path, so will I spread My Word in every nation to englobe you all in My Transcendent Light so that when you walk, your going will be unhindered - as you run you will not stumble. I love those who love Me, those who seek Me eagerly shall find Me! I have given you My Heart to love: so love Me and I shall do great things in you. ♥

Little one, My Return is closer than you think; I am coming My Vassula to reign in every heart. I have listened to you, do not let your heart be troubled or afflicted because nothing will come between you and Me. I ask you, My beloved and My bride, to have constancy and faith so that you grow in Me. I bless you, live in Me.
♥ IXθΥΣ ⤛⊂◯⊃

I WOULD MAKE MY WORDS A FIRE IN YOUR MOUTH
WILL NOT ONE OF YOU RESTORE MY HONOUR
BY RESTORING MY TOTTERING HOUSE?

May 1st, 1992

My Lord Yahweh, my Beloved Father in Heaven, Your Name is an oil poured out. You have revealed Your Name to me by coming forward to me and saving me. You brought me up bringing me near You.

Yahweh my God You have redeemed me.

Ah Vassula, though you were a dried up driftwood ready to be thrown on the fire to be burnt, I came hurrying to you to save you. In the valley of Death I have found you, making Me plunge into mourning. My Cry turned the heavens in a state of alarm; the very memory of that sight still deeply grieves Me, such was the distress I endured. I was patient with you for many years, I called you many times then but you would not listen; but, greatly loving, I did not make an end of you, I have shown you instead My Faithfulness in your wickedness. The pain and injuries you were giving My Son were devouring slowly My Mercy. So great was your guilt and so many your sins that I was ready to avenge My Son's Wounds by striking you. Ah Vassula, your Mother of Perpetual Help cried at My Feet, shedding Tears of Blood for you - yes, your Holy Mother favoured you and comforted Me... My Heart was deeply moved and My anger was removed by Her Tears; the tempest that had risen in Me was silenced. I, Yahweh, your Eternal Father, loved you with an everlasting Love since that day I created you and held you in My Hands. Ah... never will I forget that day how small you were. I said: 'I will drive the Invader away from many souls through this small and delicate girl.' You and I then made a pact together, that you would work for Peace proclaiming My Love to resound to the ends of the earth, and that through your weakness I would rally those who would be on the point of perishing. I would make you fearless to threats and of invaders and through you I would pursue and track down the renegades; then, in you I would bring your generation to reconcile and unite. Since I was to encroach on My Enemy's plans already, I had to bring your soul to consent with Me and strengthen you from the beginning. I said: 'sanctify yourself already and fast from your birth, this is what I desire: I shall not give you light at your birth[1] for three days and for three nights you will remain in the dark; this is how you will fast.' So this is why I swore to widen once more the space in your heart for My entry and like a tempest I came upon you to destroy everything that rendered My Heart into a Wound; I blew like one blows on the coal fire, this is the way I blew in your soul to enliven the extinguishing flame inside you. I said: 'let your flame now rise in your darkness to rejoice My Soul, let your aridity turn like a watered garden, like a spring of water' and with everlasting tenderness I have pressed you on My Heart, making you Mine again. I swore to change your rebellious and unruly heart into a resting place for Me. I made you understand that I should be your only God, your only Love unrivalled and irrevocable; I then removed your veil to honour My Name and declared openly to My Celestial Hall that I Myself will fight those who will fight and persecute you, for now, I, your Creator will be your Husband and your only Refuge. I would be He who confides in you and you in Me. I would make My words a fire in your mouth to proclaim them to the ends of the earth - all that you have learned you have learned from Me. I, Yahweh, your Eternal Father embellished you, delicate little girl; I stoop at this very moment, down to you to lift your soul close against My Heart. ♥

My affliction My child, to watch My children refusing My Love, My Peace and My Graces are turning My Heart over inside Me. I need souls to comfort Me, I need generous souls to appease My burning wrath. Be My relief, be My Heaven. I

---

[1] When I was born my eyes were stuck together, they were shut. I opened my eyes only after 3 days. My mother filled with fright that I might be perhaps without eyes asked and prayed to our Saint Paraskevi (a Greek saint for the eyes) for help and vowed to give me her name after Vassula. Paraskevi in Greek means: Friday.

12

Yahweh, love you all. Come, I will show My Glory through your nothingness. For My Sake, put an end to transgression, put a stop to rebellion. You are all parcelled out and are constantly failing your fruits to unite and live holy. Are not you and your brothers all the same to Me? Will not one of you restore My Honour by restoring My tottering House? Will I be forced to draw My sword on you? Will you continue to resist My Holy Spirit? Will you continue recrucifying My Son? The Amen is asking each one of you to bless your enemies, to forgive them all and come and reconcile with Me, your God, so that you will be able to reconcile with your brothers, to make one single Body for My Glory. Come and make Peace with Me; let everyone hear Me and understand by reading Me, how I, your Eternal Father, am rendered every time My Eyes watch from Heaven sights that lacerate My Heart and how I can conquer the bitter plague that invades more and more in each soul. I am the Amen and I can save you if you turn to Me.

Vassula, your race is not yet over, but I, Yahweh your Eternal Father am with you. Be blessed for allowing Me to use your hand and your time. My Finger is on your heart so that you remember who fostered you. ♥

CONSECRATE YOURSELVES TO MY SACRED HEART
MY CROSS WILL BE THE SIGN BETWEEN YOU AND ME

May 5th, 1992

My child, I give you My Peace. ♥ *Write: I am your King, and I am here to mark a Cross on the foreheads of all those who are sincere and who truly love Me. You are to say with Me the consecration of My Sacred Heart[1] and while you are saying it, I will with My Finger, be marking you with My Sign.* ♥ *My Cross will be the Sign between you and Me, and I will love you with all My Heart, and I will guard you and fragrance you with My Fragrance.* ♥ *Consecrate yourselves to My Sacred Heart and to the Immaculate Heart of your Blessed Mother, so that I may be able to make out of your hearts My Garden, My Resting Place and My Palace.* ♥ *Come back to Me with all your heart; do not come and stand before Me with a divided heart, come to Me and I shall leave a blessing on you while you pass Me by. I am your Hope so open your mouths to invoke Me with your heart and I shall fill your mouth so that you praise and honour Me.*

---

[1]Consecration dictated to me by the Sacred Heart on January 26th, 1992.

My sons, My daughters, be gentle with each other, love one another as I love you so that in the Day of Judgement you may find favour before Me. I tell you, the days are coming when the unripe fruit will be of no use anymore, for your King who speaks to you today will reveal His Glory and you will see Him face to Face. So blessed are those who are ready to receive Me, they shall be called heirs of the Most High. ♥ *Be one. Ecclesia shall revive!* ΙΧθΥΣ ✝

Our Blessed Mother speaks:

Children of My Heart, you are in these days watching the world tearing itself up, knocking itself down. The earth is overthrowing My children, destroying them and bringing disaster after disaster in many families; the foundations of the earth are rocking from the evil it produced. I tell you, so long as you continue to allow the Evil one to enslave you to Him many will be buried in the dust of sin. I ask you, and I implore you to bury all that is not holy. How long will you hesitate to set out to find Him who loves you most? Your Husband and your Creator? He who gave you your redemption and His Heritage. The Kingdom prepared for you since the foundation of the world calls you all day long. You can become the builders and the planters of this generation. You can become the menders of this earth; repay the earth's guilt by fasting, by sacrifice and by prayers from the heart. Happy the peacemakers: they shall be called sons of God. ♥ **Receive My blessings.**

FOR PRISONERS

May 6th, 1992

"He has walled me in; I cannot escape; he has made my chains heavy." (Lm 3:7) Compassionately, however You come to their room to pasture them. (Message for all the prisoners of the world.)

Peace to you. It is I, the Lord, your Redeemer; do not be astonished, it is My Holy Spirit who dwells in each heart who speaks to you. My Love for you is beyond knowledge and not until you are in Heaven will you be able to understand its fullness. ♥ *I descend in these days of darkness from My Celestial Throne, all the way to you, to allow you to know as well what is happening and what I am doing. I am coming to reassure you all of My Promise; I come to reassure you, little children, of My Love and My Faithfulness to all of you; My Return is very near. I tell you solemnly, whoever keeps My Word will never see death* ♥ *and you who hesitate, doubt no longer but believe. If you had failed to understand the*

14

teachings of scripture do not let your hearts be troubled. Come today and confide in Me, heart to heart. Which father would hear his child's lament and not have every fibre of his heart broken? I am your Eternal Father, He who loves you with an Eternal Love and like a father who invites his children to share and inherit his property; so am I calling you to be heirs of My Kingdom. Ah... would that these words of Mine were inscribed on your heart and absorbed by you... My little children, you heard Me say: I am going away but I shall indeed be with you soon. I tell you truly I am with you soon. I have said that there are many rooms in My Father's House, each one of you has a room. Give your souls peace and rest by filling in this room; fill them by making Peace with Me. Today Satan is vomiting all his hatred on the earth; he tears up and overthrows countries in his rage; he destroys and brings disaster after disaster, but with great power My Hand shall build up all that he has torn. Everything I have written in My Hymn of Love to you is only a reminder of My Word. It is to refresh your memories and to tell you with My Heart in My Hand that I thirst for lack of love. I do not bear a grudge against anyone; you are all My seed and I, I am your Eternal Father and Companion. I know well what is in your mind but I am not here to accuse you for your deeds. I am here today to show you how Compassion and Tenderness were treated. In My Heart I still have the lance's blade and a Crown of Thorns surrounds My Heart, the pillars of the heavens tremble at this sight and all My angels cover their faces in agony; the very moon lacks brightness. Your God is being recrucified hour after hour from men's wickedness and spite. A Path was traced out with My own Blood to redeem you and if your feet have wandered from this Rightful Path, I tell you, I have come all the way to you now to take you by your hand and guide your steps back in this Rightful Path. Offer Me your will, abandon yourselves to Me and allow Me to tear down the wall you have built across My Path which prevents you and Me from meeting. ♥ *My little friends, your Holy One still has many things to say to you but they would be too much for you now. I will only add one more thing: if I have come all the way to you in your cell, it is because of the greatness of the Love I have for you.* <u>Call Me</u> *and I shall hear you. I bless you leaving a Sigh of My Love on your forehead.* IXθΥΣ ⸻⟨⟩

MY LOVE HYMN WILL GROW INTO A RIVER
AND THIS RIVER WILL GROW INTO A SEA OF LOVE

May 15th, 1992

It was You my Lord who gave me true education of many of Your Mysteries, since You Yourself fostered me and are my guide of Wisdom. Your Wisdom made me to be intimate with You. "Grant me to speak as You would wish and express thoughts worthy of Your gifts." (Ws 7:15)

I Yahweh love you. Remain near Me, remain near Me and walk with your Father.
♥ *Repeat after Me this prayer:*

O Eternal Father,
Author of the Love Hymn,
King from the beginning,
You rose, God, to say something
to all the inhabitants of the earth.
True to the greatness of Your Mercy
and of Your Name,
You rained upon us blessing upon blessing;
Over the waves of the sea
and over the whole earth
Your fragrance travelled.
Mighty God,
there have never been such lovely things
before in our generation.
Author of the Love Hymn,
Your Works are superb ornamentation,
magnificent, adornment to delight
the eye and the heart.
I mean to praise You, Eternal Father,
all my life
and sing to You my God
as long as I live.

Amen.

and I tell you: spread My Love Hymn with Me, your hand in My Hand. Little one, walk with Me, it pleases Me. I intend in the coming days to irrigate My flower beds. Wait My child and you shall see My Glory. My Love Hymn will grow into a river and this river will grow into a sea of Love.

> *"I shall make discipline shine out, I shall then*
> *pour out teaching like prophecy, as a legacy to*
> *all future generations." (Si 24:32-33)*

16

Yes, this is what I say, I, the Creator of the heavens and the earth. And know that soon My whole purpose will be fulfilled. City[1] after city will be inhabited by Me and rebuilt.[2] I will raise your ruins and reconstruct My altars[3] one after the other. The ban once lifted, then all mankind will be consecrated to My Sacred Heart and the Immaculate Heart of your Mother. Ecclesia shall revive.

THESE ARE THE LAST DAYS OF MY MERCY

May 28th, 1992
Detroit, Michigan

Vassula, let no one take away the prize I have given you; before you I Am. Pray for the proud that judge My Works[4], they have no love for Me in them. Daughter, honour Me by proclaiming My Messages in all these assemblies, there is very little time left. These are the last days of My Mercy, so stay awake, stay vigilant; do not allow Satan a foothold; do not allow your spirit to judge prematurely; rid yourselves of carping criticism so that in the Day of Judgement you will not be judged.

I am the Light of the world. Be prepared for I may come into your house anytime now; down from the heavens, from My royal Throne, I shall soon descend in your dreadful night. Little children, be at Peace. I give you My Peace; be patient just for a little while longer and continue to glorify Me with your love. I love you all with all My Heart, I love you - you are all My seed. I bless you leaving the Sigh of My Love on your foreheads. ♥

---

[1]That is: soul after soul.
[2]That is: converted.
[3]The faithful who were persecuted and wounded.
[4]Jesus was referring to the opposition that came up in Detroit. There was a certain small group of people who accused me of being a 'new-ager', belonging to the new-age sect. They went in every one of my meetings to 'boycott' the meetings, distributing to all the people flyers with an article against me.

MY CROSS WILL LEAD YOU TO SANCTITY
AND INTO YOUR ROOM IN HEAVEN

May 29th, 1992
Detroit, Michigan

Jesus?

I Am. Open your heart and receive Me. Tell My people that I shall come to them soon. ♥ *On that Day every inhabitant in this world will know that I Am who I Am. Pray for those who dispute what you teach. Pray and do not allow your hearts to condemn them. Have faith in Me and trust Me - Love is near you. Glorify Me by restoring peace where there is dissension; love where there is hatred; imitate Me your Lord in this age of darkness; embrace My Cross - My Cross will lead you to sanctity and into your room in Heaven.* ♥ *Love will embrace you.*

IXθYΣ ⋈⊃

CONSECRATE ALL YOUR DAYS AND NIGHTS TO PRAYER,
SACRIFICE, PENANCE

June 5th, 1992

Little one, single-minded, defend the Truth to death. Continue to give yourself to Me, your God and consecrate all your days and nights to prayer, sacrifice, penance. Offer Me your will and the Enemy will have no chance to approach you. Keep the sound teaching you have learned from Me and do not worry when your accusers calumniate you. I call to unity from My Cross, so never lose confidence, for it is I, the Resurrected One who calls everyone. It is not you, it is I, the Christ and your Redeemer who calls his scattered sheep.

Vassula be gentle and patient with your accusers for they know not what they are doing. By loving them as I love you, My child, and by giving yourself up as a sacrifice, you will be pleasing to Me. Through your sacrifice I will have My House restored and many souls brought back to Me. ♥ *You, who are less than the least of all My children, have been entrusted with My Cross of Unity; My Cross of Unity is heavy but you are to bear it with love and patience. Be My Echo and proclaim to everyone the Infinite riches of My Sacred Heart.* ♥ *You are to proclaim that Unity will only be built on love and humility. Remain loyal to Me, your Lord, and remember that My Father created you precisely for this purpose - to give glory to*

18

Us.[1] ♥ *So stand your ground and do not sway with the tempests - I am beside you. Do not be afraid, the Truth will speak up. Yes, My loyal helper, you will receive from My Spirit all that I have to say. My words, My child, will be like a lamp shining on the sacred lamp-stand, they shall be like a sword in your mouth; I shall open your mouth to speak without fear. Take courage, My child, I Myself am taking up your cause. Listen, today your accusers are covered with confusion but you will escape their sword, here[2]... this is your Refuge, see? This is where you are... I am your Strength, your Stronghold; although the scourge falls on your back incessantly, do not lose heart, remember how I voluntarily gave My back for your salvation without complaint. It is you My priest, that the world will reject because you are attesting the truthfulness I have given you. ♥ You do not speak as for yourself, no, the written words are My Own, your Abba's. I live in you and you in Me, you are My temple and I live in you and now that I have clothed you I shall remind you once more: no servant is greater than his Master. If the world has not known Me who am Master and God and My Own people did not accept Me although I came in My domain, would the world today recognize and accept anyone sent by Me? Never! I have said these things to you, My child, to remind you that if the world persecuted Me they will persecute you too, if they wounded Me, they will wound you too, if they jeered and mocked their King, they will mock and jeer all his household too and if they crucified Me, their God, they will drag you too to Calvary and have you crucified. ♥*

Vassula, your race is not finished... offer Me your life like a good soldier since I have enlisted you in this Holy Battle to fight against error and to be a threat to Satan and all his empire. Do not be afraid of the sufferings that are coming to you; be brave under trials; be patient like I am patient. Today Satan is deceiving many of you; the man of deception is among you, spreading his errors to an ignorant and somnolent lot because they preferred their own pleasure to Me their God. Some keep up the outward appearance of religion but have rejected the inner power of it: My Holy Spirit. So then, anybody who is My servant and comes from My household, is certain to be attacked but, My loyal helper, soon I will bring you safely home, in My Heavenly Kingdom. Pray and sacrifice, pray and sacrifice. Look at your wretchedness now and then, that you may not fall into temptation; never feel satisfied with yourself; look at your misery so that it keeps you alert and awake; despise yourself and humble yourself so that I may lift you always up to Me and perfect you. Satan is powerful, yet not for long. Hope, My Vassula, praise Me and glorify Me. It is I, Christ, speaking in you. IΧθΥΣ ⤳⟖

---

[1]The Holy Trinity.
[2]Jesus with both of His Hands showed me His Heart that was like on fire but a golden flame.

WHOSE LOVE AMONG YOU IS STRONGER THAN DEATH?

June 10th, 1992

Peace be with you. ♥ *Love loves you. Flower, listen and write: like a man who invites his friends to share his meals, I invite you today to pray but also to share with Me My sufferings, My joy, and My desires.* ♥ *You are waiting anxiously to hear Me and listen in silence to what I have to say, and ah!... how I know how thirsty some of you are!*

In these times, as never before, I reach down My Hand from above, to save you from the powers of evil who are prepared to blow out the little light that is left in you and force you to dwell in darkness. So do not say: "there is no one to save me and no one to befriend me" and that help is denied you. Invoke Me with your heart and I will come flying to you...

I am your Friend ♥

I am He who loves you most; I am the All-Faithful. I have taught you not to refuse a kindness to anyone who begs it; will you refuse to pluck the thorns that pierce My Heart? For this I need generous souls. I need today more than ever victim souls; is there among you any sensitive soul left? Who among you will set Me like a seal on his heart? Whose love, among you, is stronger than Death? Have you not yet understood how I am sick with love for you generation? Open to Me entirely your heart, My sister, My brother, My beloved ones for My Mouth is dryer than parchment for lack of love. Abandon yourselves to Me; why do you fear in surrendering? You will only be surrendering to your Holy One, to the One you say you love. Give Me your heart entirely and I will make a heaven out of it to Glorify Me, your King. Consecrate yourselves to My Sacred Heart and glorify Me. You are all of My Household and I do not wish anyone to be lost. If you remain in Me you will live. Continue, My little lambs, to make known to your brothers and your sisters the consecration to My Sacred Heart as well as the consecration to the Immaculate Heart of your Mother. I bless you all leaving the Sigh of My Love on your foreheads. ♥ ΙΧθΥΣ ⋊⃝⃗

Message from Our Blessed Mother:

Beloved children, do whatever Jesus tells you; give thanks to His Name for His Faithful Love; lift up your heads towards God and you will grow radiant. My poor children, I look from above in your cities where there is no rest and where there are so many upheavals; I look, but I cannot find enough love nor generosity. ♥ I need more prayers, more generosity and love to help you. I find so very few to support me in My prayers. ♥ Renounce all your evil ways and live holy; I need your prayers like a thirsty soil needing rain, to help you and embellish you for My Son. There must be no further delay now. The Enemy is determined to kill mercilessly and without pity and continue to thrust people out of their own country. I have seen horrors from above and My Heart is broken within Me but I can restore the lands and I can restore Peace among brothers only if you will be alert to My supplications of Prayers and My Calls to sacrifice. ♥ Loss of children, widowhood, at once will come to an end. Take this time Our Messages to heart. Offer yourselves to God and He shall take you by the hand and form you; He will make out of you a reflection of His Divine Image. ♥ With Him you will learn that suffering is divine, mortification appeasing in God's Eyes, obedience pleasing to Him. Desire what is mostly rejected by this world:

His Cross

I bless you all with My Maternal Love. ♥

EVERYWHERE MY EYES TURN, THEY SEE TREACHERY

June 16th, 1992

This morning, I was tempted and had a small doubt that God was really speaking to me.

> "Yahweh, let my words come to your ears, spare
> a thought for my sighs. Listen to my cry for
> help, my King and my God."
>
> Psalm 5:1-2

Vassula, I Yahweh love you. Remember My child how distressed I was[1] when I was telling you then about My children abandoning Me? ♥ Vassula, tell Me, where have you acquired this great stock of wisdom in Scriptures if it were not from Wisdom Herself who smiled on you and became your personal Teacher?... Vassula, I am your Abba, let Me tell you: in the beginning you lived for one purpose, you lived for yourself, you served your vanity; you believed then that you were vested in splendour and glory but in reality you were quite naked. No one had come to tell you how naked you were until I, Myself, came to shine on you

---

[1] Message not yet published dated 19th September 1986 from the Eternal Father.

and in your darkness; only then, your eyes for the first time saw yourself in the Light of the Truth, you saw yourself as you really are. If it were not for My Compassion a sword would have awaited you. However, I pitied you and in My Mercy, I breathed in your nostrils reviving you; I then restored your memory to our relationship. ♥ I did great things to you:

I espoused you to Me and you
became Mine.[1] ♥

I then formed you to become a child after My own Heart who would carry My whole purpose: <u>to bring back My people to the real faith based on Love and share the Cross of My Son, the Cross of Unity</u>. ♥ I have formed you to live not for yourself but to live for Me; I have taught you, My child, how much greater it is to serve My House than to serve your vanity. Now, spend your life with Me, for this is the lot assigned to you in life and in this Era of Great Apostasy; so whatever work I propose to you to do, do it wholeheartedly for one purpose - to glorify Me. The world is somnolent and runs grave risks since it does not know what is going to come to them; out of their sin their apostasy will bring death to them. No one can tell when My Day comes; this hour will come suddenly upon them. Today I have done great things to save you, I planted Vineyards everywhere, I made gardens and orchards out of deserts. I am a Father afflicted by untimely mourning because I watch how more ready this world is to kill than to love; massive child-murdering initiations erupt daily. Everywhere My Eyes turn they see treachery, murders, corruption, adultery, fraud, disorder in marriage, people who sneer at religion, pollution of souls, perjury, sins against all nature; how then am I to keep silent? This is why Justice will overtake this lot. ♥ Here I am speaking openly like a Father, anxious but offended and afflicted. My Voice is groaning from the Heavens, hear Me: is there any upright man left among you?...

Suddenly God's Eyes turned towards me, He stopped abruptly His dictation.

Vassula, go and do your other duties too, I am aware of your time and of your capacity. Beloved of My Soul quench your thirst in Me; I Am a Living Fountain of Purity and I love you. Come, We[2] bless you, come.

---

[1]Allusion to Isaiah 54,5. "For now your Creator will be your husband, his name, Yahweh Sabaoth."
[2]The Holy Trinity spoke.

YOUR GOD IS COMING

June 17th, 1992
(Continuation of the message of 16th June 1992)

Little one be with Me - are you ready?

Yes Lord.

Hear Me then: how long am I to be offended while you will not listen, to cry 'repent!' in your ear generation, and you will not hear? But look I am stirring up the dead, these worthless people whose behaviour was appalling and far from sanctity. The world shall be filled with My Knowledge and My Glory, for as the waters swell the sea, My Spirit too, like a tide shall come in and no one will be able to stop My Spirit from flowing in. Vassula, pray with Me:

> *Lord, in Your Strength and*
> *in Your Wisdom You raised me,*
> *You fostered me; in Your Love*
> *You helped me, and I*
> *became Your bride. Lord,*
> *You confided Your*
> *Message to me;*
> *praised be the Lord.*
> *Come Lord, maranatha!*
> *Amen.*

and I tell you: I am on the Path of Return. Like a traveller who left, I, Jesus am well on the road back to you.

My Lord, tell me all about it, it makes me happy!

My child I have spoken once... I will not speak again. ♥

What do You mean My Lord?

My words are clear...

I still do not know what You mean, Lord.

Look, My child, your God is coming! Love is coming, He is coming to live among you. ♥

Tell me more about it Lord! We all delight to hear <u>Hope</u> speaking where there is despair; <u>Love</u> pronouncing where there is hatred; <u>Peace</u> announcing where there are wars and conflicts.

Courage! Do not be afraid or saddened, for these few days left. Trust wholeheartedly in Me; be strong, stand firm. Yes stand firm and I shall make your voice carry as far as the clouds proclaiming My Message. Approach Me, approach Me...

THE HOUR HAS COME, THE HOUR OF MY HOLY SPIRIT TO GLORIFY MY SON'S BODY

June 17th, 1992

Yahweh my God, You who are so tender and so close to me hear the sufferings of He who is the Delight of Your Soul: Jesus Christ, Your Son. The Church's gateways are all deserted and her priests groan for her desolation. The City once thronged with the faithful sits in loneliness as if suddenly widowed. Your temples[1] are perishing one after the other as they search for food to keep life in them but what they inhale instead of incense is Satan's smoke. Where are the domains like a garden? Where are the blossoming vines that gave out once, their fragrance? Why are Your altars broken?[2]

Peace My child, peace... hear Me: the Great Day is near you now, nearer than you think. ♥ Altar, tell everyone that I will show My Glory and display My Holiness through and through; I will pour out My Spirit without reserve on all mankind. Your eyes have seen nothing and your ears have heard nothing yet. Today your hearts are sick and your eyes dim because you are living in darkness and desolation and the Enemy roams to and fro in this desolation. I, the Lord, will multiply the visions on your young people and many, many more of your sons and daughters shall prophesy - more than now. I will make up for the years of your aridity that led you to apostatize; I shall send My Spirit without reserve to invade My domains and with My Finger I will rebuild My broken altars; and My vines with faded leaves looking now like a garden without water, I shall come to them to irrigate

---

[1] We are the temples of God.
[2] The three questions concern the soul. Domains, vines, altars, are our soul.

with My Spirit. I will remove the thorns and the brambles choking them, and My vines will yield their fruit. ♥ *I will do all these things to save you. I will display portents in heaven and on earth as never before; I will increase the visions; I will raise and increase prophets; I then will send you My angels to guide you and I the Holy One will live in your midst.* ♥ *My people are diseased through their disloyalty. They refused the gifts of My Spirit because they trusted in their spirit, not Mine, making treaties with their mind; but now the hour has come, the hour of My Holy Spirit, to glorify My Son's Body. Come, Vassula, I want you zealous, I want you to love Me. So My child, I will instil in you fervour and a few drops of My burning Love to enliven you with My Flame.*

I SHALL MAKE THE PROPHECIES OF ISAIAH COME TRUE

June 18th, 1992

Vassula, let Me sing the rest of My Love Hymn to you, let Me stretch My Love Hymn for the sake of those who were not ready to hear.

Yes Lord! Come and melt our hearts, show us my King, my God, the Riches of Your Sacred Heart. Show us the Light in Your Face. Let us understand that You, my God are looking down from heaven to see if a single one is left with faith, with love, and if a single one is seeking You. Blessed be Your Name, blessed be our Lord, our Redeemer, Emmanuel, for He has sung to us His Love Hymn, even as He proclaimed by the mouth of His prophets that He would return, thus He prepares us now for this encounter. And You, Blessed Mother, You who gave us our Redeemer, once more You are with us preparing the way for the Lord and preparing us to meet Him. And the Lord out of His Infinite Mercy will visit us to give us light in our darkness and guide our feet into the way of Peace, Love and Unity.

> "Glory to God in the highest heaven, and peace
> to men who enjoy His favours."

Luke 2:14

My Vassula, I shall come to a people who never gave a thought for Me, never a glance for what I have done to redeem them and I shall make the prophecies of Isaiah[1] come true: "I have been found by those who did not seek Me and have revealed Myself to those who did not consult Me" and the valleys of death with its dead and its ashes will be consecrated to Our Two Hearts. ♥ *Be in Peace. Come*

---

[1] Isaiah 65:1.

and repeat after Me these words:

Jesus be my support,
without You I am nothing,
without You
my table is empty,
without You I am defeated.
Be my Inspiration and fill me.
Be my Refuge and my Strength.
I love You and my
will is Yours
so be it.
Amen.

THIS IS MY BATTLE

July 2nd, 1992

Our Holy Mother:

Christ is soon with you. You labour My child, but anything you offer My Son for His Glory will sanctify you and will glorify Him. It was God's purpose to reveal Himself to you for the sake of His Body, the Church. Daughter remember, Jesus will never, <u>never</u> fail you. Remember how you entrusted Me with the Messages you are receiving? I, as your Mother, guard what you have given Me and today like yesterday I will continue spreading quickly My Son's Messages. Satan may sound virulent and may appear as through he triumphs over every nation and that his victories are glorious, but Vassula, soon I shall conquer him, <u>for this is My battle</u>. Daughter, I shall comfort you and give you sufficient strength to continue your mission. ♥

The Lord speaks now:

Please Me and announce My Words everywhere I send you. Stand firm. Lean on My Heart and feel loved. Tell My children to consecrate themselves and their families to Our Two Hearts. ♥ Consecrate yourselves so that I mark you as Mine.

Hear Me: I tell you solemnly that there will come a time of distress like never before; the earth is already seeing the dawn of this time. Stand firm and do not allow yourselves to be deceived. Many are claiming that they hear Me proclaiming messages but I am not the Author of these messages, nor your Mother either. I have already warned you of these times; I have many times warned you that in these times many false prophets will arise, to ruin your Master's Works with lies. The ears of those who hear will be alert; the heart of the hasty will be deceived. ♥ (Many will try to deceive you Vassula, saying that I, Jesus am sending them to you, but they are false prophets). Remember many false Christs will rise; some will produce great signs and impress even the elect. ♥ There, I have warned you again. Daughter? Will you allow Me to continue this Work in you? Pray so that you may not fall into temptation. I shall open the way for you, do not fear. My Love for you is Eternal. ♥

July 3rd, 1992
Mexico

I am your Holy One coming down from Heaven to drench you all with the dew of My Love; oh that the heart of mankind turns from wickedness! I give you mighty signs of My Love but who is there to acknowledge My Love? Mexico! Your King is here to take you in His Arms.

I am here

stooping down to you to whisper in your ear the greatness of My Love. ♥ Have you not understood that Our Two Hearts were the Ones looking after you? Our Two Hearts are here to settle in your homes and protect you from the fierce anger of Satan. ♥ Today I am calling your nation more than ever to set your hearts for Me, your Lord. Every little one of you is so very precious to Me. Come, come and love Me; moisten My parched lips with your love. I will heal all the disloyalty in your nation and your King will give you rest. ♥ I bless each one of you and tell you from the core of My Heart.

*Love loves you
be one in My Love. ♥*

ΙΧθΥΣ ⊃⊂▷

CONSECRATE YOUR COUNTRY TO OUR TWO HEARTS

July 7th, 1992
Mazatlan - Mexico

We have failed to appreciate Your great Love and we do not cease to defile Your Holy Spirit, who now tries to adopt us and bring us to the Truth based on Love. Apostasy has intermarried with rationalism that gave birth to atheism. We have failed You and are continuing to fail You. Some are deliberately challenging Your Holiness. You are speaking but who is listening? Grief wastes away Your Eyes, yet all You receive is contempt.

Peace be with you. ♥ *Pass on My Peace to My dearest soul.[1] You must believe Me when I say that My Holy Spirit in your generation's great apostasy is persecuted like never before; He has become the stumbling block of your era. I have said, My little children, that they will expel you from your Father's House and condemn you thinking they are doing a holy duty to Me! Do not let your little hearts be troubled, My beloved ones. I, your Redeemer, am before you. Today, I speak for the sake of all those who are wounded: I give you My Peace, let this Peace envelop you, do not fear and do not say, "what am I to do Lord?" I tell you: pray without ceasing to sanctify your own soul and those of others; pray with your heart and make the demon flee. Be united to Me and no one and nothing will come between you and Me; the time has come when you should not hesitate any more. Spread vineyards wherever you can; do not fear of the tempests that arise now and then. My Sacred Heart is your Refuge, so come and consecrate yourselves and your families to Me and to the Immaculate Heart of your Mother. I, Jesus, intend to remain in your country and sanctify it, for this I ask you to consecrate your country to Our Two Hearts. I bless you all out of the depths of My Heart.* ΙΧθΥΣ ⤳

---

[1] Father Masi of Mazatlan, Mexico.

I SHALL SEND YOU TO A FEW MORE NATIONS

July 8th, 1992

"There was a vine: You uprooted it from Egypt to plant it. You cleared a space where it could grow; it took root and filled the whole country. Your Message covered the mountains with its shade, Your cedars with its branches; its tendrils extended to the sea, its offshoots all the way to the river. Please, God, look down from heaven, look at this vine, visit it, protect what Your Own Hand has planted."

Psalm 80:8-11/Psalm 80:14-15

Lord?

I Am. Little one lean on Me. Vassula of My Sacred Heart, rejoice! Your King has come all the way to your doorstep and into your room; your King has stooped down from above to reach you. Step by step I have taught you, I am your Educator. Little by little I have drawn you away from the world to plunge you into My Heart; I have revealed to you things beyond your knowledge and your capacity. Believe, My sweet pupil, I Jesus love you. Have My peace, we will work together. I and you will spread My Message; I shall send you to a few more nations, then when I feel you have accomplished your mission you shall return to Me. I, Myself, shall come and fetch you.

α ☧ ω

I AM YOUR BEST FRIEND,
YOUR DEAREST HOLY COMPANION

July 10th, 1992
Villeneuve, Switzerland

"There in front of the throne they were singing a new hymn in the presence of the four animals and the elders, a hymn that could only be learnt by the hundred and forty-four thousand who had been redeemed by the world."

Apocalypse 14:3

Lord?

I Am. I am speaking, so do not doubt. Vassula of My Sacred Heart, allow Me to write a few lines for this afternoon.

Dearest friends, I have come all the way from heaven to sing to you My New Hymn of Love and remind you all of My faithful Love:

I am your best friend
your dearest Holy Companion.

All along I have been by your side, and although I have been many times ignored I remained with you to make you feel My Presence. Every time you were about to rebel against Me, I, the Lord, full of Compassion, grasped you by the right hand to draw you in My Heart and show you My Infinite Love. <u>Blessed of My Soul!</u> Alone you are not; I am always with you to console you and guard you as one guards the pupil of his eye. ♥ Do not say, 'there is darkness all around me' I am near you to lead you out of this darkness, you need only to say: '<u>come Lord</u>!' and I shall be flying to you, My child.

Day and night I am waiting for your abandonment, do not delay; abandon yourselves entirely to Me so that you may be able to be in My Light. ♥ If you love Me you will allow Me to do what I think best for you. Do not fear, offer Me your heart and I shall place it into My Sacred Heart to consume it. If you love Me as you say, you will sing to the nations My new Hymn of Love, to glorify Me and raise a new life for each soul. My Heart to you I have offered. Will you offer Me yours in turn? Love is by your side and with the Sigh of My Love on your foreheads I bless you and your families. Be one. IXθΥΣ ⋈⬤

Our Blessed Mother:

I am by your side to console you, but I too, who am your Mother need your consolation for great is the anxiety of My Heart. Many of My children are rebelling against the Most High. I need your prayers; offer Me your prayers for My intentions. Vassula, tell them to live as children of God. ♥

SPIRITUAL GUIDANCE FROM JESUS

July 14th, 1992

Lord, the first time I was persecuted I could not even present my defence; there was not a single witness to support me. Everyone of them deserted me, but You Lord stood by me and gave me strength so that through me the whole Message might be proclaimed for all the nations to hear; and so I was rescued from the Lion's mouth. The Lord will rescue me from all evil attempts on me, (and oh are they many!) You will in the end bring me safely to Your Kingdom. To You be glory for ever and ever. Amen.

2 Timothy 4:16-18

My Vassula, lead a life in peace. Love Me and propound My Peace everywhere I am sending you; have you not yet understood My Power? So what is there to fear? I have put My Finger to your lips; you are not completely conscious of it, yet I tell you, My Finger is on your lips to pronounce all that I Myself have given you. No, you will not get by unscathed but I have enough Power to cure you and heal your wounds. My Cup tastes bitter yet out of Love I invited you to share it with Me. If I were not standing by your side, you would have been torn to pieces, so do not worry, no one can snatch you from Me. ♥

Hear My advice: do not get worn out. Zeal for My House devours you and I am happy for your enthusiasm to glorify Me, nevertheless the Bridegroom says to His bride: prophecy in peace and allow My Holy Spirit to be your Guide. My Holy Spirit will not saddle you with weights beyond your strength, therefore, do not prolong the requests and the meetings, My Spirit will direct you so that you may give them sufficient, only the essential should be done. Serve in humility, preach and teach all that I have given you; in this way you will glorify Me. Take care about what you teach, repeat only the words I Myself have given you; do not add nor subtract; be dedicated to Me. I am reminding you of these things so as to proclaim in perfection My Knowledge. ♥ I want you to be My Echo so that those who are listening may recognize My Voice. Be careful always to choose the right course.

Vassula, My Bride, the race is not yet over; do everything though in peace. I want My bride near Me, under My dictation, now and then, work in harmony with Me. ♥ I am sending you to reap a harvest I Myself worked for, therefore, remember, console Me, desire Me, thirst for Me in My stillness and allow your Saviour to rest in you. I Jesus bless you. ΙΧθΥΣ ⤙⟊

JUDGEMENT DAY - THE TIME OF SORTING HAS COME
THE LAMB'S SEAL

July 20th, 1992

My flower, I Jesus bless you and give you My Peace. ♥

I have been asking you all from the beginning to lead a holy life since I am holy; I have been asking you, dearest ones, to change your lives so that you inherit My Kingdom. When My angels who had been given supreme authority rebelled against Me and destruction took the best out of them, My Justice did not spare them, they were thrown down to the underworld to wait for the day of Judgement. They too will be judged before the very eyes of everyone, and ah!.... what a terrible sight that will be! I will judge <u>everyone</u> according to what he has done and not done. In front of My Throne everyone will stand in silence and in awe for the Day of this final Judgement will be so dreadful that it will make everyone tremble with fright in front of the Supreme Judge that I Am. You will all see a huge number of fallen angels who were driven out of heaven and fought in bitterness and spite, Michael the Archangel and his angels. Yes, your eyes will see My Rivals, the Rivals of the Holy One, of the Anointed One. You will all see those fallen angels, adepts of Lucifer, the primeval serpent who tried to lead my sons and my daughters all astray. ♥ *You will see multitudes of those who defiled My Name and transgressed My Law, those who refused to be reared and fostered by My Holiness and preferred to be labelled on their forehead by the Deceiver...[1] Yes, Vassula, a harsh vision has been shown you. I tell you: I will soon come with My saints to pronounce judgement on the world and to sentence the guilty. Today My Grace is being revealed to all mankind to renew you all with My Holy Spirit before My Day and remind you of My Law.* ♥

I will in that Day repay everyone according to what he deserves. I have said that I will severely punish anyone who insults the Spirit of Grace and treats My Spirit as foolish; that is why you should stay awake. Today more than ever before, I am asking you all to consecrate yourselves, your families and your nations to Our Two Hearts. Allow Me to seal your forehead with the seal of My Holy Spirit. <u>The Time of sorting has come, the time of reckoning is here</u>. I said to everyone that I shall come as a thief upon you; when I return no one will be suspecting anything; then, of two men one will be taken, one left; of two women one will be taken, one left. The Harvest is almost ready to be reaped and countless corpses will be left when I say:

---

[1] I was here given a vision of this multitude of fallen angels standing in front of God's Throne in the Day of Judgement. It was awesome, and sad.

"I Am here!"

Then I will say to My angel:[1] "the hour has come to sort out and pull out all who are not Mine. Sort out from those who acknowledged Me, all those who have not willed to comply with My Law; sort out from those who allowed and welcomed My Holy Spirit to be their Guide and their Torch, all those who rebelled in their apostasy against Me;[2] sort out from those who are branded on the forehead with the Lamb's Seal, all those with the name of the beast or with the number 666." The time is here and I Myself am branding My people with My Name and My Father's Name. ♥

Vassula, I did not open the floodgates of heaven to pour out My blessings in abundance for you alone, but My blessings are being poured upon all mankind now before My Great Return. You are, as I have been saying, living in a time of great mercy and grace, but the Day is coming now, burning like a furnace; and all those who have not been sealed with My Name on their forehead will be like stubble in this Day. I am revealing to you what is to come before I break the sixth seal.[3]

Come and consecrate yourselves to My Sacred Heart and to the Immaculate Heart of your Mother. As I have said, you are living in a period of Grace and Mercy. Daughter, just as you changed from being disobedient to Me and have reconciled making peace with Me and enjoying now mercy, so will it be for those who are still rebelling against Me. ♥ *I will show My Infinite Love and Mercy to all mankind before I send My four angels at the four corners of the earth[4] whose duty it is to devastate land and sea. I have ordered these angels to wait before they do any damage on land or at sea or to the trees until I have branded My Seal on the foreheads of those who have complied with My Law[5] of those who benefited from My Graces and of My Mercy, to these I say: serve and do not wait to be served so that My Father in heaven allots you a place in His Tent. By being faithful to Me you will undergo great persecutions, but have I not promised you white robes in heaven? Have I not promised you that you will no longer be hungry or thirsty?[6] So do not fear when the tempests rise against you, Scriptures are being accomplished. Happy are you who die in Me the Lord! I shall indeed reward you.* ♥

---

[1] Allusion to the parable of the darnel. (Matthew 13:24-30)
[2] This passage confirms St Paul's prophecy in 2 Thessalonians 2:1-12. The 2 foretelling signs of the end of times: The Great Revolt (Apostasy) and the Rebel (spirit of Rebellion).
[3] Apocalypse 6:12-17.
[4] Apocalypse 7:1.
[5] Apocalypse 7:2-3.
[6] Allusion to Apocalypse 7:9-17.

My child, Love is near you and My Spirit upon you; <u>Hope</u> My child is found in My Sacred Heart; <u>Love</u> My own is given to you freely, and <u>Faith</u> is a blessing from Me. ♥ *My Spirit rejoices in your nothingness and My Soul delights in your frailty; I have raised you to console Me and delight Me. I have chosen you by grace to quench My thirst of Love; nothing to do with your merits since you have none.* ♥ *Are you ready, My child, to please your Saviour?*

Yes Lord, I want to please you!

At any cost?

At any cost. All that I have as good <u>is</u> Yours. You are my ever Faithful God, the Holy One.

♥ *I will lead you with a sensitive hand and I will breathe over you to spread My sweet smell around. Be attentive when I speak, My pupil, I have pushed back a legion of demons who were heading to plunder My property.[1]*

Praised be Jesus!

Come, daughter, we shall work. Be united with Us.[2] ♥ *We, us?*

Yes!

SIMILARLY, MY HOLY SPIRIT WILL DIRECT YOU AS I HAVE DIRECTED MY DISCIPLES

July 21st, 1992

Lord?

I Am. I give you My Peace and I bless you. Flower, let us work - write:

I tell you solemnly, I am giving the world many signs but are they ready to recognize My heavenly signs? Many today only speak about what they have seen, but yet reject the evidence of My Holy Spirit so manifest now. Similarly, My Holy Spirit will direct you as I have directed My disciples, overshadowing you all with

---

[1]Me.
[2]Jesus and our Holy Mother.

My compassionate Love. I will show everyone that My Name, Jesus, means He-Who-Saves.

Daughter, turn your gaze on Me and flourish; I am all Bountiful. I invested you with My Knowledge and I have entrusted you with My Interests. Your Maker has encircled you with His Powerful Arms, so do not fear, I will hurl down your enemies who in reality are My enemies. Your Holy Mother is your Defence. I the Lord shall make you strong to carry My Message to the four corners of the earth. Night and day I watch over you, so do not trouble your little heart, I shall from today open more gates for you. From today, priests, bishops and cardinals will begin to open their ears and hear My Voice. ♥ They will begin to listen and with a shower of graces poured on them coming from My Infinite Mercy they will begin to understand, and from their eyes the scales encrusted by the dust of Apostasy will fall and they will once more begin to see the Splendour of My Holy Spirit. They will perceive the Fathomless Riches of My Sacred Heart, these Riches reserved for your times.

Daughter, consider yourself as a baby just weaned from your Maker; remain small so that I may easily lift you to My Breast and press you on My cheek. ♥ All wisdom from men will decay and the shrewdness of your generation shall be shrouded. ♥ My Heart is with you. Daughter, you will continue witnessing and being My Echo to this apostatized generation who are on the point of collapse; you will be My ambassador for My Affairs. I will, My child, carry you on My Shoulders in the heart of a nation who preferred to trust in wile and guile than in the Breath of My Holy Spirit. I will send you now to these who have taken Me the Holy One out of their sight. I will bring them a conversion and a salvation such as was never heard of before nor seen before. I will rescue this nation, spare it and save it. In that day the song they shall sing to Me will be like that on a wedding night. I will send you to them[1] as a pilgrim. ♥

> *"I will make the blind walk along the road and lead them along paths; I will turn darkness into Light before them and rocky places into level tracks. These things I will do, and not leave them undone."*
>
> *Isaiah 42:16*

I will come to save them.

---

[1]I immediately realized then that Christ meant Russia. I was invited to go as a pilgrim.

BY THE ROAD THAT I CAME ON I WILL RETURN

July 22nd, 1992

Lord, so long as we remain unreconciled we continue to desecrate Your Holy Church, and slowly but steadily continue to reduce our souls to a pile of ruins. Are we truly seeking You when we talk about UNITY? When are You going to intervene and bring us back to our senses to seek You earnestly? Are we using our tongues to lie outright to You pretending only, we want to UNITE? How long will we defy You and You will not intervene? We are repeatedly challenging You, when are You going to challenge us?

Pupil, repeat after Me this prayer:

> *God, You who are full of Compassion,*
> *let Your Face smile on us to unite us.*
> *Look down from heaven,*
> *look at our division*
> *that reigns now in Your Church.*
> *Your lambs, My Shepherd,*
> *are perishing in great numbers as*
> *they search to pasture to*
> *keep life in them.*
> *Listen to the groans of the Church;*
> *this great Apostasy predicted is*
> *robbing You of Your children.*
> *Bring to Your Church this*
> *Day of Glory You once foretold*
> *so that we may all be one.*
> *Lord, do not remain silent*
> *and do not delay any more,*
> *Come! Come, bring to us the*
> *Day once foretold, make everyone*
> *hear Your Majestic Voice.*
> *You are known to be Gracious*
> *My God,*
> *give me a hearing and answer me...*
> *I give You thanks*
> *for I know that You have heard me.*
>
> *Amen.* ♥

Yes My Vassula, trust Me wholeheartedly; put all your faith in Me, I shall never fail you...[1] pronounce what you have to pronounce!

Lord, where else could I put my faith and my trust? You are the Holy One who decides, You are Omnipotent so where else would I go?

Yet you are free to choose, even if you turn to be unfaithful, I am always faithful.

Come, write: I reprove the man who behaves like a stranger to Me. I will set My Throne in your hearts to honour My Holy Name and I will shine My Magnificence in your little hearts. The time is almost up now; I am coming to your help. I am coming to your oppressed; <u>by the road that I came on I will return</u>; I will enter My City in Glory. I am coming, therefore be ready to welcome Me O children! I am calling <u>you</u>! My cries go out to all of you and the foundations of the earth are shaken from My Calls. How long do you intend to sleep? When are you going to rise from your lethargy and apathy? Disaster is at your very doors and will overtake you in your sleep, suddenly, irretrievably, and you will still remain unaware? But look, look Who is leaning all the way to you, knocking at the very doors of your heart. Open to Me, My own, for My Sacred Heart is lacerated for lack of love, My Lips parched and with blisters for lack of Love. Open to your Holy One and console Him as He will console you. I am at your doors - do not refuse to accept Me... If you allow Me to enter your heart I shall make a fountain spring inside you because your soul would have acknowledged Me as your Saviour; I will water your so pitiable desolation and like a branch of the Vine you will flourish and bear fruit.

Come, daughter, I Jesus bless you for allowing Me to use your hand. ♥
ΙΧθΥΣ ⊂▷

YOUR WHOLE LIFE SHOULD REVOLVE AROUND ME

July 23rd, 1992

Jesus?

I Am. Love Me more. Vassula, are you prepared? The Spouse then will continue engraving in you His Work. You and I are united in My Love, are you aware of this?

---

[1] Jesus looked at me gravely and said what followed.

Your Breath blows on me telling me that I am counted as one of Your children, although my spirit still weak and uncomprehending remains perplexed at Your choice.

Creature, your Creator is with you incessantly; do not reach out for anything else but Me, I am with you. ♥ Creature? Your whole life should revolve around Me, your life is in My Hands and you are nothing but a speck of dust. Desire Me. Today I made you taste the sweetness of My Love and the warmth of My Heart. ♥ Dearest soul, enter into this Heart that loves you and R-E-M-A-I-N there. ♥

TO KEEP YOU ALIVE I HAVE OFFERED YOU TO EAT MY BODY AND DRINK MY BLOOD

July 27th, 1992

Vassula, My wretched bride, I had foreseen all your failures and your weaknesses well before you were born. I knew all along that the one I had set My Mind on to cast out in the corruption of the world to be My Net, would wriggle and twist in My Hands. I knew how the devil would place crafty traps to trap she whom My Heart loves, therefore, do not be astonished and do not think that I am astonished either... Do you still want to continue bearing My Cross I so lovingly offered you?

Yes, I do. Do not hide Your Face from me nor Your Cross. Your Holy Face looking on me will give me the strength I need to carry Your Cross. This is all I need. I do not deserve that the King of kings so lovingly looks down at me from heaven.

Vassula, do not make Me change My Mind about your singleness of heart[1] for carrying out the task I so favourably offered you. Your spirit ought to be <u>united</u> with My Spirit, your heart with My Heart, and in this perfect union you will be able to be My Echo. ♥ Look! Courage daughter! Your Loved One is coming soon, to end up the sorrows and laments of this earth. Listen, daughter, have I deprived you of anything?

---

[1]This was a reproach from Jesus.

No, Lord, You have done only the opposite:

You filled my mouth
with Celestial Manna,
You nourished my soul,
You have done great things for me.

Yes! I have offered you a full table. I have offered you My House, My Heart and Myself. I have offered you to live with Me, in My Light. I have offered you from the Palm of My Hand My Celestial Manna. I have offered you, while crossing this desert, part of My Cloak. <u>To keep you alive I have offered you to eat My Body and drink My Blood</u>. I have accustomed your steps to walk in My Steps. I have instituted in you My favours and the Riches of My Sacred Heart. I have held back legions of demons who were ready to tear you apart. Like a Warrior I fought and defended your cause from the Deceiver. I have poured on you and on your household My blessings. I have restored your house[1] from ruin and death. I have so lovingly pressed your lips on My Wounds and shared My Cup with you; and like a Spouse offering His matrimonial bed I have offered you My Cross, My Thorned Crown and My Nails to sanctify you - What more could I have done to you that I have not done?... Vassiliki[2] do not give in to the promptings of your nature lest you lose your fruits and are left like a withered tree. ♥ I have courted you, Vassiliki, with all My Soul and with all My Soul I intend to keep you forever Mine, yet I will from now on demand much more from you than before. If you do not stand according to the demands of My Sacred Heart you will face double your crosses. Remember, you owe your life to Me and your salvation too; keep your distance from the world that has got everything but Me. May the Strength you receive from Me open your mouth and proclaim My marvels; may every race in the world hear My Message. I shall sow everywhere and in each country, I shall cultivate your deserts and the sound of My Footsteps will be heard by all the inhabitants of the earth, to the far ends of the world. Daughter, treat Me tenderly and I shall offer your soul delights and consolations to appease your thirst. Get up at midnight now and then to praise Me and thank Me for the favours and the blessings I so lavishly poured on you - you are dear to Me. Look on My right side and see who is with Me... yes, your advocate and your Mother, guarding you from peril and from threats. Like a lamp shining on the sacred lamp-stand[3] She shows you the Way to Me. ♥

---

[1] That is: "restored your soul."
[2] Jesus gravely called out my official name of birth.
[3] Si (Ecc) 26:17.

July 28th, 1992
On my way to Rhodos, Greece

Lord, fortify Your city[1] against seige, fortify Your sanctuary since I have to face a people who say to the seers, 'see no visions' to the prophet, 'do not prophesy the truth to us' and to Your predilected souls, 'you are damned.' Have they not read, 'every kingdom divided against itself is heading for ruin; and no town, no household divided against itself can stand.' (Mt 12:25) And if it is through Satan thousands are being converted through Your Message 'True Life in God', a Message given by Your Spirit, a Message anointed from Your Mouth, through whom then do their holy priests convert?

And so I tell you again and again, every one of men's sins and blasphemies will be forgiven, but blasphemy against My Spirit will not be forgiven. Anyone speaking against My Holy Spirit and he will not be forgiven either in this world or in the next[2] and you, do not let your heart be troubled, I am with you. Come My Vassula, I and you, you and I together, see? Have My Peace, we, us? Come.
ΙΧθΥΣ ⊂▷

August 2nd, 1992
Rhodos, Greece

Blessed be the Lord, my Rock who trains me as His personal pupil.

Vassula, love Me and propound My Love. This is your Lord speaking, the One whom you say you love. I bless you My child. ♥ ΙΧθΥΣ ⊂▷

August 6th, 1992
Rhodos, Greece

(I have been asked to witness on the T.V.)

My friend, My little friend, do not hesitate announce My Message and feel

---

[1] That is: fortify my soul.
[2] Matthew 12:31-32.

confident - I Am is with you. Seek the Riches of My Sacred Heart and promulgate My fragrance. My Heart is an Abyss of Love. Have My Peace and receive My Spirit; honour Me and glorify Me. ΙΧθΥΣ ⊳⊂⊐

THE SPIRIT HAS ANOINTED THESE MESSAGES

August 9th, 1992
Rhodos, Greece

(After a rain of persecutions after I had spoken on the T.V., calumnies and blockages. Many conversions and repentances were made, during the program. But then a fire was lit by a monk, who combats the Lord's message.)

Vassula, My Call has awakened many dead hearts; I shall speak for the sake of all those who are standing around you. Remain in Me more than ever and do not fear, so much have I written to you about My Love. Whoever keeps faithful to Me will not be uprooted by the tempests, but he who would leave the world to overcome him will lose My Heart. ♥ The Spirit has anointed these Messages; the Spirit is Truth, therefore no one will be able to obstruct the Truth. I have levelled a path for you, so pray that you may proclaim My Message as clearly as you ought to. ♥ Take My Hand and walk with Me; dearest soul, I Am is your Holy Companion. All I have to say for now is: courage, be blessed, and be united. Pray in your tribulations; all the saints are with you. ♥ We, us? Come. ΙΧθΥΣ ⊳⊂⊐

DO NOT BLAME THE PROUD, PRAY FOR THEM

August 9th, 1992

O Lord! Hear my prayer, listen to my cry of help, do not stay deaf to my crying. (Psalm 39:12)

Faith My child; have faith in Me and trust Me. Sorrowful you must never be when persecuted. How long will it take you to understand Me? Look, I Am is leading you and I am known to have overturned kings and whole kingdoms when these became an obstacle for My passage; I have exalted the lowly and overpowered the haughty. Come, do not blame the proud; pray for them. ΙΧθΥΣ ⊳⊂⊐

THE OPPOSITIONS IN RHODOS

August 10th, 1992

O Lord, why is there so much obstinacy? O Lord, I am starting to learn that great names do not give wisdom. There was a time when I hoped for much from their mouths when they proclaim the words: UNITY and RECONCILIATION, but I do not even see the dawn of it either...

Peace be with you. The sound of your bitterness did not escape Me. Have I ever told you I will abandon you?

No Lord.

So why do you worry? I created you for this mission. Come, look at Me, you will always have good things to eat with Me and your table will always be full when you are with Me. Creature! I will lead you on the way that you must go; retreat into My Heart when you need to rest. Do not lose your courage; Wisdom will instruct you. Devote your time to Me and I will use you for My designs; I will use your mouth to be as sharp as a two-edged sword when you pronounce My Words. I intend to teach sound judgement to the ignorant. If you allow Me to use you I will carry out My Plan. Until everything has been performed and has been carried out My fervent desire of unity and reconciliation among you all will <u>not</u> diminish. I have put on paper through you how I desire you to unite; from the very beginning I have spoken clearly. Vassula, My child, have you not read that even a small amount of yeast is enough to leaven all the dough? Therefore, do not give Me any premature judgement. ♥

MY CHILD, PROPHESY!

August 20th, 1992
Rhodos - Greece

Dear and faithful child, while you are weak I am King. Here I am sending you back to your own to remind them of My principles.

Some of you have become mild and tepid for you have welcomed My words without trust when you gather together in My Name - woe to those who sell My Blood to honour their name! Woe for those who are satisfied now and direct their lives by their natural inclinations and ignore My Spirit! Woe to those who will become an obstacle to the door I Myself have thrown open to announce My Message. Woe for those who believe they act wisely with the world - they are servants of the world, not Mine. They are slaves of the world and espoused to hypocrisy, corruption and all that My Heart abhors. You say you suffer injustice for the sake of My Name, rejoice! For My Day will soon dawn upon all of you with fire; rejoice and be glad when people accuse you and disgrace you publicly exhibiting you as a spectacle of disgrace for My sake and My Message. All the greater will be your reward in heaven for having endured with love the insults of the world. Pray so that your chains that still bind you to the world may be unbound by Me. Pray for those who cannot tell their right hand from their left hand. No one is worthy of My Call so do not blame the proud. Grace now is upon you and Mercy is enveloping you. Your King has offered you His Heart wholeheartedly but I have noticed that not everyone has offered Me their heart entirely; not everyone is willing to comply with My principles; no, not everyone has gone according to My Heart's desires but has listened instead to their own voice - that which is their own law because of their weak faith. To these I say: pray that you may not lapse from My favour, pray that you will do My Will. Let My words spread now and do not be subject to your human thinking. ♥ I have three more questions to ask: why have you reduced My Voice?

What have you done with the Messages I have chosen to be read?

Where has the man once so eager to please me gone?

Father! Forgive them for they know not what they are doing!...

My child prophesy! Let your mouth with My words be like a sword... serve Me, Love is near you.

Lord, what if they do not do Your Will?

Then I shall withdraw My Heart, My favours and My graces but My Cross will remain. ♥

(This message was given to those who laid blocks on the passage our Lord had opened. Temptations, fear, doubts led certain people not to trust and rely on the plan God had prepared for Rhodos. Jesus warned them.)

WHERE THERE IS DISSENSION GIVE PEACE AND LOVE

August 22nd, 1992
For the group of Rhodos

Lord?

I Am. All I ask from you is peace. Where there is dissension give peace and love; where there is confusion ask for My Light. Ask!, ask and I shall give! Respect each other and do not allow your hearts to harden; do not give Satan a foothold. Be calm and offer Me your prayers; how many prayers am I hearing? Pray and fast so that the evil one leaves; pray more. Remain in Me, like children depend on Me. Pray, pray with your heart. ♥

My Ways are not your ways, so do not give way to your own mind. Little do you know how I proceed. Seed everywhere and wherever you can; I know your capacity and I know where I am sending you. Blessed are you who are calumniated and ridiculed for My Sake, I tell you, you will not be unheard when you cry out My Name. Peace. Pray and lean on Me; ecclesia shall revive!

ΙΧθΥΣ ⋉▭▷

THEY SHOULD NOT PUT ME TO THE TEST ANYMORE

August 23rd, 1992

(Locution very early that morning.) I heard Jesus tell me after I had been praying to Him: *"I am happy that you are taking time so early in the morning to talk to Me. Tell them* (the group of Rhodos) *that My Heart is an Abyss of Love. Tell them that they should not put Me to the test anymore."* (And that they should read 1 Corinthians 14:26-32)

Later on:

O Lord Jesus Christ, to Your most Sacred Heart I confide this intention:

Help us and shepherd us,
give us Your Peace, Son of the Eternal Father,
lower us, so that Your Eyes, King of
the Heavens, may look
down from above.
O Beloved Son of our Father,
do not allow multitudes to be crushed,
men are dying of corruption,
speed Your Work O Holy One of the Father
and may Your Return be hastened;
You who are the Delight of the Father,
do not allow the world anymore
to defy the glorious Presence
of Your Holy Spirit.
My eyes are turned towards You O Lord,
and my heart takes its refuge
in Your Sacred Heart
to obtain Peace and Love,
do not leave me defenceless!

Amen.

I have made you fearless of men - this is My doing. In My Day I shall have an answer for those who taunt Me now. As for you My daughter, I find My delight in your nothingness.

The Son of your Father

tells you: I shall continue to spread out My Messages. Those who oppose Me will run into the Cornerstone and will be crushed.

The Delight of the Father

tells you: I am doing a great Work that no man can stop, and as for those who charged on you bitter accusations I tell you, their hands will drop and their plans will not work out. ♥ *My Heart is consumed with longing for your love generation, and is ablaze like a burning Furnace. I love you all with all My Heart, with all My Heart I love you! Behold, I will pour out My Love to you all to adorn your wretchedness.*

Lord, how is it the world has become so corrupt?

Have you not read: where there is no guidance, a people falls.[1] The mouth of the perverse brings forth no wisdom, yet he who perverts will be found out. Nothing remains hidden in My Eyes, but in these days of Mercy My Hand is still stretched out for anyone who will cry out repentance - they shall be rescued. Love is near you My little loyal friend. The Amen blesses you. Come and worship Me. I Am.
♥

August 26th, 1992
Greece - Island of Simi - Panormiti
(Panormiti is St Michael)

I went and stayed four days on a small island called Panormiti. Only very few houses are there with a predominating Monastery and Church of St Michael. His icon is human size all covered in silver. It is a miraculous icon. I felt called there, so I went to pray and ask St Michael for his intercession. Before leaving for Panormiti that morning at 8.00 am Jesus came to me in a dream-vision. He did not allow me to look at Him. He wanted me only to feel Him. He stood at my right side and just then He put His left Arm around my shoulder. Immediately I felt God's warm consoling protection. My soul rejoiced! He allowed me to touch His left Hand which held me. I felt each of His Fingers. Then He allowed me to touch with my left hand His Heart, His Beard, then part of His Holy Face; every one of those seconds put my soul in an indescribable consolation, peace, joy and reassurance. He did not need to talk. His Presence so close to me was telling me everything. I AM is with me.

Later on that day:

My Peace I give you - be patient as I am patient. The Father loves you and has entrusted you with this mission. Do not think that I am not aware of its weight; I am your Spouse who will provide you,[2] console you and remain faithful to you. You are the writing tablet of the Father and on this tablet the Father's and My Hymn of Love is being written. Do not assume that the Most High cannot find a way to carry out His Plan among your people,[3] He will come back to His Vineyard with Fire and make an end of the tenants who have been given freely His Vineyard and given it to others because they have not kept It but made a desolation

---

[1]Pr. 11:14.
[2]Jesus reminded me of the vision; His Presence.
[3]To face the Orthodox in Greece and talk about unity this summer was as if UNITY will never be. I felt very discouraged. God made me the "go-between" to bring everyone together. It is not easy.

out of It. I have been trying through the years to warn them by sending them My servants but they killed each one of them.[1] Today in truth I tell you: 'the stone which the builders rejected proved to be the keystone.'[2] Today My Holy Spirit of Grace is the cornerstone and anyone who falls on that stone will be dashed to pieces; anyone it falls on will be crushed.

I have given you all a strong warning; do not put Me to the test any more and you daughter, do not be surprised at the reluctance your people have. No prophet is ever accepted in his own country. Were that possible then they would not have turned today into your enemy simply by having been truthful to them. Come, I bless you and your companions. ΙΧθΥΣ ⤷⬤

MESSAGE FROM SAINT MICHAEL THE ARCHANGEL

August 27th, 1992
Simi - Panormiti

Vassula, listen to My Archangel whom you came to visit:

Child of God, do not fear, stand firm when they persecute you. You are not alone. Give your True Shepherd all your problems and He will guide and lead you and the Mighty One has His Hand on you. Listen when He speaks for He has great plans on you. He is the living God and there is no one above Him. I shall help everyone who is willing to overcome the Evil One and in the Father, through the Father, I will undo the work of the devil. Let anyone who wants to boast, boast of the Lord! Praised be the Lord. Remain in His Heart and remember, He has truly spoken to you ♥ - God's Archangel Michael.

---

[1]Here I understood that God has <u>been</u> sending chosen souls with messages to them (the Greek priest, monks) but their incredulity 'killed' the Spirit.
[2]Psalm 118:22.

ANYONE WHO BLASPHEMES AGAINST MY HOLY SPIRIT WILL NOT BE FORGIVEN

September 7th, 1992

Faithfulness is the essence of Your word and Your word is integrity itself. Our life is in Your Hands, and yet our liberty is ours. It is Your Gift to us. But what have we done with our freedom? We used it to ensnare ourself and made out of it a destructive weapon for our soul. We need Your Holy Spirit to intervene, that ever-flowing Source of River water let it gush now on us.

Ah Vassula... the paths of this generation will in the end be straightened and men will be taught faithfulness and integrity - just wait and you shall see... As long as you live and there is breath in your body, I will shepherd you; I will keep instructing you in the fullness of My Wisdom; I shall guard you against stumbling. I, the Most High, have favoured you - be happy soul, be happy! Listen now and understand: there is no poison worse for the soul than the poison of blasphemy to My Holy Spirit. Anyone who blasphemes against My Holy Spirit will not be forgiven - so be on the watch that you may not find yourselves blaspheming against My Holy Spirit. That is why My Wisdom says to you: beware not to apostatize and reject My Holy Spirit of Truth who descends to you in these days to revive your lethargy. In My days on earth they hated Me for no reason, yet on the Cross I asked the Heavenly Father to forgive them. Today if the world rejects My Holy Spirit of Grace and mocks Him calling Him evil or foolish they will find themselves unrepentant when My Day comes. You who received a share of My Holy Spirit once, would fall from Grace and you shall not be renewed a second time. How would you since you would be unable to repent with your heart and I will be coming and will still find you unrepentant, with your heart hard as stone, dry and without fruit..?[1]

I will have to cut you and throw you to be burnt.

Therefore, in all truth, I tell you, <u>open your hearts</u> and understand how My Holy Spirit blows anywhere He pleases, and breathes freely in My envoys. ♥ Recognize them by their fruit and do not be slaves of your mind. ♥ Every soul should know how mockery, jealousy, carping criticism, judgement and calumny opposes the Holy Spirit of Truth. You should be awake and praying not to be put to the test. I say this to you today: if your lips should cause you to sin, fast then with your lips[2]

---

[1] Jesus suddenly stopped here then very gravely said the following words.
[2] Jesus means to give a vow of silence.

rather than have your lips condemn you and your soul burn with agony.[1] You must love your neighbour as yourself. You will say now: but You have given us this command already; yes, I have, but have you followed it? Pray and ask for My Holy Spirit to come and rest on you!

Vassula, let My Holy Name be always on your lips and in your heart. I am your Educator and My favour is upon you. Console Me and let your heart be My heaven; realize who I am. ♥ Pray with joy and I shall court you; praise Me and I shall envelop you with My imperishable Light; bless Me and satisfy My Heart and I Myself shall come to you and carry you across My threshold into My House. Yes, just like a Bridegroom carrying his bride across the threshold, I too will come delicately with great tenderness and love and carry you to show you My Throne of Glory. I have sent you My Holy Spirit from above to rest on you and teach you what you have never heard of, to save you and millions of others. Remain near Me, My sweet disciple, our journey is not yet over, we still have a mile to go to teach the rest of My children the knowledge of holy things.

I shall deliver you to many nations to honour My Holy Name and on you will be written My Knowledge; I shall grant you to speak as I would wish you to speak. ♥ Let now your heart rejoice and treasure what I have said to you, never fail Me. Love Me and absorb Me. I am Love. ♥ IXθYΣ ⊱⟐

I AM THEIR (RUSSIA'S) MOTHER

- PROPHECY -
I WILL DELIVER YOU (RUSSIA) AND PLACE YOU AS HEAD OF MANY NATIONS

September 9th, 1992

Our Holy Mother:

Peace be with you. Tell My children of Russia that I Myself will train them spiritually. I am their Mother; I am the Woman of the Apocalypse. Russia, My daughter, be patient - the smell of death will not spread any more. Indeed your sufferings are soon coming at an end, for the Lord in His Mercy will lift from you the shroud of death that had enveloped you so many years. Your eyes,

---

[1]Jesus means in purgatory.

Russia, My daughter, are soon going to look on your King, your Saviour in all His Splendour, who is known by the Names: Faithful and True. Your King is on His way of return. Russia, listen to Him:

[1]Those who are far away will come and repent. They will rebuild My Church and I for My part will anoint each heart, and as someone roused from his sleep, Russia will rouse quivering with impatience to be consumed by Me. I will deliver you and place you as head of many nations.[2] Foreigners will grow faint of heart upon seeing your beauty. Your right hand will be in My Hand. I will lift you high above everyone else and I will perform My pleasure in you; your Maker with delight and great joy will display your beauty to His people,[3] to His angels and to all His saints and the heavens will declare openly their joy. The vault of heaven will proclaim My glory at the four corners of the earth. ♥ Russia... you were dead, and I had put sackcloth on to manifest My grief and like a father mourning his child, I went about dejected and sorrowing; now I have selected you among many nations to manifest My Glory through you. Soon, your Holy Mother will topple Satan's throne to the ground and crush the Serpent's head. Loss of children and widowhood at once will end. The dragon will be handed over to his fate and the world will have a period of peace. ♥ The Mother of all humanity will prevail in the end and I, the Lord your God, will triumph in every nation, in every heart and in every race.[4]

THE EARTH SOON WILL SHAKE AND WITH A ROAR THE SKY WILL VANISH

September 9th, 1992

My daughter, the world is offending Me daily, lacking reverence to My Holiness; they misuse the freedom I have given them by destroying themselves. This generation has become an unsightly blot in My Eyes; they repay evil with evil - this is why I shall not spare this generation. No one can say I have not warned them;

---

[1]Our Lord now speaks.
[2]Spiritually I think.
[3]Jesus had a happy Voice and His Face had a happiness. He appeared as a father lifting up in the air his child.
[4]This last passage means that all the peoples of the world would recognize Jesus as the Christ. The Lamb. Allusion to Apocalypse 6:15-16.

no one can say I have not been patient. The earth soon will shake and with a roar the sky will vanish leaving everyone in total darkness and with great violence the elements of the earth, the mountains and islands will catch fire and wear out. Every blade of grass will burn and in front of Me you will stand, disarmed, generation. The power is in your mouth to cry out to Me and repent but you prefer to be homeless and err in sin, you prefer to live in deserts.

> Lord, I feel your Sacred Heart so grieved. You will tell me to feel sorry for my brothers and sisters instead. I do, but I also feel sorrowful for Your sadness for Your Heart is lacerated. With Your grace my Lord You can turn anyone acceptable in Your Eyes, you can make us ready to do Your Will. I, who am as You said the least of least, have been entrusted with this mission with Your Grace, why not others? I have been given a free gift, Your Grace, why can't others receive it too?

You are bold Vassula, to inquire My Wisdom.[1]

Perhaps I am bold, but it is because I know how Your Heart feels. It does not please You either to punish us and abase us.

Everything that comes from earth returns to earth.[2] The sins of your generation have pierced all Eternity, they have pierced My Heart. Pray and intercede, My Vassula, that there will be still time to mark as many as I can with My Seal before My Day, for good and bad will suffer in these days.

A ☧ Ω

MY MESSAGES ARE MY GIFT TO YOU ALL

September 10th, 1992

Lord, my God!

I Am. ♥ *Little one, I am the Author of the Messages: 'True Life in God' - they are My gift to you all; they are to make you understand My Heart and how I stand by you always and everywhere.* ♥

---

[1] Majestically Jesus pronounced these words.
[2] I understood that we are self-destructing ourselves by our apostasy.

IF THEY HAVE CALLED THE MASTER
OF THE HOUSE BEELZEBUL,
WHAT WILL THEY NOT SAY OF HIS HOUSEHOLD?

September 11th, 1992

Peace be with you. Daughter, what I shall ask from you today are the following:

- *deny yourself longer from food.*
- *rest when you must and do not save your rosary for midnight!*
- *go to confession more often; do not say yes and then not do it; it is better to say 'I will try to please you Lord.'*

Your King is aware of your capacity, the depth of your wretchedness and your amazing weakness. Pupil, your Teacher will not deny you of His Light, He will give you enough Light to grow and follow the footprints of your Teacher and what awaited the Teacher will await the pupil. Have I not said, "the disciple is not superior than his teacher, nor the slave to his master; it is enough for the disciple that he should grow to be like his teacher and the slave like his master; if they have called the master of the house Beelzebul, what will they not say of his household?" (Matthew 10:24,25)

If My own relatives believed I was out of My Mind[1] what would you not hear then from only your friends? Come, embrace My Cross and learn from your Master; My Soul rejoices every time I hear you pray. ♥

---

[1] Mark 3:21.

OUR TWO HEARTS, IN THESE LAST DAYS
HAVE BEEN OUT TEACHING YOU
SO LONG AS YOU REMAIN DIVIDED
YOU ARE STILL IN THE DARK

September 14th, 1992

Jesus?

I Am. Little do you know how much I prayed for you to the Father, let alone your Holy Mother! My Eyes stream with Tears daily because of the crimes of this world... My Eyes are worn out looking for generous souls. ♥ *My Heart is troubled and My whole being shudders with pain to the point that I refrain to look down on this generation's sins lest My Cup brims over. I have made a new hymn of Love[1] to sing to you and reach each heart from the heavens to save you and remind you of My Eternal Love I have for each one of you. I have spoken from above, not to impose My rules on you, but propose to you an alliance of Peace and Love to lead you all under My Wings and unite you. <u>I proposed to wed you...</u> but how many of you understood what I had been saying? Have you really understood what the Spouse had offered you? Explain then to Me why every time I speak of <u>reconciliation</u> you turn your eyes away from Me... I was a stranger and you did not welcome Me, I was at your door knocking and you did not hear Me; though I have spoken the Truth, your tongue never ceased to tell foul lies about Me, judging Me and condemning Me. I have come to teach you good sense and remind you of My Knowledge, leadership and service, but you mocked Me and jeered at Me; I visited you with love and tenderness with a yearning to unite you all in My Heart and teach you all over again the rules of My primitive church, but you allowed your own rules to invade your spirit throwing Me out of your heart. You will ask: "when, have I done all these things to you Lord?" I tell you, you have done them already to Me - you judged Me prematurely and allowed your lips to condemn Me, for what you have done to My envoys you have done it to Me. You profaned their name, thinking you were doing Me a favour, but in reality you were profaning My Name. How can you still say: "Your Word, My Lord, is a lamp to my feet, a light on my path" when you have not received My Word nor reconciled with your brother?*

With great Love and Tenderness Our Two Hearts, in these last days, have been out[2] teaching you all over again that prayer, love and humility are the KEYS to your salvation, but how many of you have really penetrated this Truth? Your heart

---

[1]These messages.
[2]Allusion to Apocalypse 11.

is the gateway through which I can enter to heal you and guide you in My Path. Have you really treasured Our Words in your heart <u>or are you still out for war</u>? You cannot hide from Me nor can you say I have deprived you of the Truth. Explain then to Me, if you claim you are in the Truth, your division... Open your eyes My friend! Open your heart, <u>not</u> your mind! I tell you again:

There is not a good man left, no, not one really, there is not one who understands since all of you are under sin's dominion, not one who looks for Me; all have turned aside, tainted all alike and yet many of you claim to be in the light. I tell you, so long as you remain divided you are still in the dark; so long as you rejoice in your division, you are still not knowing where you are going because it is too dark to see. I have come to you to offer you a free gift, the gift of My Love, but Love again was misunderstood, rejected and alien in your heart. In spite of all My pleas to reconcile you and unite you, you go on sinning - how can I forgive your sins when you are repeatedly repressing My Words? You hear My Voice but you no longer recognize It; unless you allow Me to uproot all that is not Me in your heart, you will never see how today My Holy Spirit seeks in you more than any time: reconciliation and unity.

<u>*I have shown you how to unite.*</u>

Unity will be in your heart; reconciliation will be in the heart and not by a signed treaty! How can any man claim he is just when your countries are at war and aflame! Learn that My Sacred Heart seeks from you:

> *charity, generosity, prayer and a spirit of reconciliation, and to love one another as I love you.*

Will I hear from you your cry of surrender and of repentance?

ASK MY SPIRIT TO HELP YOU, ASK!

September 17th, 1992

Message for those working for these messages:

My child, trust Me. You are unable to lift your little finger on your own - all power comes from Me. Reward Me now and offer Me your will ♥ *- I am waiting.*

My WILL IS YOURS!

I, Jesus, tell you: you enjoy My favour, for you are under My authority. Tell all those whom My Heart selected that I shall never fail them - the Spouse will provide their needs. Let everyone see in them true witnesses; let everyone know there is truth in them by their way of sharing. I am sending them out to face the world; they must abstain from carping criticism so that their tongue does not kill them or divide them; not one of them has earned this grace, I Jesus, offered them freely the grace, so no one should ask for money; the strong should support the weak, the rich the needy. As I have said, "there is more happiness in giving than receiving." (Acts 20:35) I will give you enough to cover your expenses so do not ever put Me to the test.[1] Be united in Me and among you; never give way to despair in your trials; do your best and I will do the rest! Courage, pray so that you may not sink; reveal the Riches of My Sacred Heart and My Glory to the world. You want to be witnesses of the Most High? Die then to yourself; you want to be one with Me? Detach yourself from the world. You want to serve Love? Follow My Footprints drenched in My Sacrificial Blood.[2] Remember one last thing: to be set free from your human inclinations and weaknesses, _ask_ My Spirit to help you - _ask!_ and it shall be given to you. I am gentle and humble of heart and I know everything in your hearts, so ask My Spirit and My Spirit _will_ come to your help; the Spirit now asks you to pray often this prayer:

> *Jesus, neither death, nor life,*
> *no angel, no prince, nothing that*
> *exists, nothing still to come*
> *not any power or height or depth*
> *nor any created thing*
> *will ever come to separate*
> *me from You. I vow to*
> *remain faithful to You -*

---

[1] Jesus means that no one should owe money to anybody or to any place.
[2] Here Jesus asks us for _real_ sacrifice.

this is my solemn vow.
Help me keep this vow forever
and ever. Amen.

... Up daughter and thresh! Let your thoughts be My Thoughts; abandon yourself to Me so that all you do will be done in My Spirit and according to My Mind. ♥ Allow My Spirit to breathe freely in you and I will accomplish My Will in you. Happy are you My child, who meditate and allow My Wisdom to be your personal Teacher! for She will reveal to you many more secrets. ♥ Receive and give, give!

DO NOT FRET AND WAIL BITTERLY WHILE BEING NAILED ON MY CROSS, TAKE ME AS AN EXAMPLE OF DIGNITY

September 25th, 1992

Here I am, to pick up my steps over these endless ruins, with a load on my back.

I come to You for consolation, for relief and now the strength in me trickles away, and I am gnawed by grief that never sleeps. With immense effort I cross the terrors of this endless Night, enfeebled by the cynicism of these false witnesses who plague my innocence all day long. It was Your pleasure to give me the key on matters my soul could have never understood alone, on marvels beyond me and my knowledge, and for this reason they hound my innocence. There, in every obscure corner they await for an opportunity to plunder my life if that were possible. They call themselves Your people, thinking their mouth is heaven, but what they proffer is false, fallacious and misleading. I am trying to be bold and show a bold face around but they are constantly gnawing on me. The godless have more charity and humility than those who claim they follow Your Law but never stop judging and have not the least hesitation to condemn, bringing misery crashing down on me. Were they godless who judge me, I could put up with that, but THEY, who call themselves Your people! People of God! To whom baptism bounds us together in Your House...

I complain, but have I not the right to unload my burden on to You Lord now and then? Yes, I know I sound and I look like a walking Lamentations Book, but I live my life in innocence, so relieve me for just a while Lord!

Vassula... do not fret and wail bitterly while being nailed on My Cross - take Me as an example of dignity. Soon the darnel will be pulled up from the wheat before

56

any one of you realizes. I have rescued you many times from the snares of your enemies who hoped to destroy you; then, daughter, why do you fear the terrors of the Night? I am only combatting inside you... leave Me alone when I am on My way to the inner room of your soul:

My Dwelling Place.

I have told you before that your soul will leap like on fire every time My Hand falls, shattering My rivals that take My place. ♥ I am Master and intend to remain your Master; I have set you as My Target for My arrows. No, Vassula, grace does not go without suffering - oh, what will I not do to My closest ones, to My dearest friends![1]

Then, allow me to take the words of Saint Theresa of Avila and tell You: no wonder You have so few friends!

All men are weak... nevertheless, I will reply to your comment and tell you: if your soul only <u>knew</u> what I am offering and doing to you, <u>you</u> would have been the one to ask Me for more trials, sufferings, crosses, the lot! - I discipline those I love so do not object to what seems good to Me; you are My jewel and like some precious stone, I cut, carve and form you into the shape I have in Mind. Therefore, I tell you, as long as you have breath inside you, you must carry out the work I Myself have given you. ♥ As for those who call themselves Mine yet are offensive when it comes to spiritual matters, I tell them: if you were blind you would not be guilty, but since you say, 'we see and can tell' your guilt remains! How many times will I have to reproach them for their incredulity and obstinacy? Come, be in Peace - I am with you for the rest of your journey. ΙΧθΥΣ ⤬⟨▷

I AM THREE TIMES HOLY

September 28th, 1992

Ah, My little pupil, I bless you; love Me and glorify Me, for I am three times Holy!

---

[1]Jesus was full of delight.

I SHALL COME SUDDENLY UPON YOU,
IN A PILLAR OF BLAZING FIRE!

September 29th, 1992

Lord, our era is guilty of grave blasphemies and, ah, Lord...

Say it!

I cannot really see the <u>dawn</u> even of UNITY!

Yes?

Maybe what You said Lord, the "soon" - it was not <u>my</u> "soon", but Yours! Yours means <u>very</u> LONG, a very long wait!

I shall come suddenly upon you, in a pillar of blazing Fire! A Fire that will change the face of this earth... Come, take courage, My child - every step you take I the Lord bless. If you have the world against you it is because you have seen My Glory; it is because I shared your meal side by side with you; it is because at your house I have entered to glorify My Name again... Have I then no right to be generous? Are you reproaching Me because I am generous with your soul? Have we not agreed that you will let Me free to do what I please with you? Come, you are weak - offer Me your weakness and your wretchedness. Ah, one more thing, unless a wheat grain falls on the ground and dies, it remains only a single grain, but My Vassula, if it dies, it yields a rich harvest... You are My adopted daughter, learn what I mean. ♥ Let your thoughts, your desires, <u>everything</u> resemble Mine! So take up your cross and follow Me. I love you to folly so love My Cross too to folly, love Me to folly. ♥

JUSTICE
HAPPY ARE YOU WHO DIE IN ME THE LORD!

October 1st, 1992

Lord, let Your Holy Face smile again on Your desolate properties[1] do not delay. Reveal Your Glory now! Many are putting obstacles to obstruct Your messages. Come!

My beloved, when your pleading began, a word was uttered and I have come to tell you what it is - do you believe that I am the beloved Son of God, Jesus Christ, speaking to you?

Yes, Lord, I believe!

Would I not then see Justice done to you, My chosen one, who supplicate Me day and night? These people are challenging My Power; when the measure of their iniquities is full, they will have to face Me as the

Judge.

Meanwhile, devote yourself to My Sacred Heart; serve and do not wait to be served so that My Father in Heaven allots you a place in heaven. In being faithful to Me you will undergo great persecutions but have I not promised you that you will no longer be hungry or thirsty?[2] So do not be afraid when the tempests rise against you. ♥ Scriptures have to be accomplished; happy are you who die in Me the Lord! I shall indeed reward you. IΧθΥΣ ⋈

MY HOLY SPIRIT

October 5th, 1992

Father, once, before Your Majesty revived the memory of my poor soul, I had forgotten who had made me. The next moment You restored my memory You asked me to lift up my eyes to the heavens, then a ray of Light shone on me and like a

---

[1]Us.
[2]Allusion to Apocalypse 7:9-17.

consuming fire, Your Spirit rested on me. True Light, Inexhaustible Treasure, You are awe-inspiring, and stupendously Great! How can I not thank and praise You, most Tender Father for resting Your Spirit on my wretched soul and making Your Spirit one with me?

Peace be with you. It is I, Yahweh, your Eternal Father, the One who taught you with Wisdom; I am the Holy One who approached you in your misery and healed you; I spoke to you in your sleep and from thereon the scales of your eyes having dropped you have seen the Light. I have taught you, daughter, not to fear Me, but to fear Me only when you reject Me and rebel against Me; I have taught you to dwell in confidence in My Presence showing you My Infinite Tenderness and the Fatherly Love I have for each one of you. I Myself have plucked your sins by the roots and in their place with the space given Me, I planted My graces in you. Although your soul leaped like on fire I had to continue My route in your soul and overthrow all the rivals who kept house with you; in My Jealous Love I replaced those rivals with abundant fruit and henceforth I became your table-companion, your delight!

Listen now, My daughter, My Own and write and tell My children this: from the depths of My Heart I call to you all! Blessed are the ones who have ears to hear; if it were not for My prophets, can you then name Me who foretold the coming of My Son? If you say you live by the Truth and in My Love, how is it then that your generation today cuts out My prophets and persecutes them just as your ancestors used to do? Out of My Infinite Mercy a City is being rebuilt for My Own people - will this City renewed be rebuilt on the blood of those you will eternally persecute?

Today more than ever I am sending you My Holy Spirit to renew you, yet for how long will this generation keep resisting My Holy Spirit? Tell Me, can a body live without a heart? Learn that My Holy Spirit is the Heart of the Body which is the Church; learn that My Holy Spirit is the Breath of the Church, the Essence of zeal for Me your God; My Holy Spirit is the sweet Manna of Heaven nourishing the poor. Happy the man who opens his heart to My Holy Spirit - he will be like a tree along a river, yielding new fruit every season, with leaves that never wither but are medicinal. Happy the man who opens his heart to My Holy Spirit, like a crystal clear stream My Spirit shall flow like a river in his heart, renewing him, for wherever this river flows, life springs up, and joy! Have you not read: the River of Life, rising from My Throne and from the Lamb will flow down in the middle of the city street? My Holy Spirit will shy away from malicious souls, but will show Himself openly to the innocent, to the poor and to the simple. With great joy My Holy Spirit will envelop these souls and become their Holy Companion and their Guide, and as they walk, their going will be unhindered; as they run, they will not stumble, and should they drink deadly poison they will remain unharmed; should they meet a legion of demons on their route, they will go by unscathed. My Holy Spirit will teach them the sweetness that exhales from Me, the depths of My Eternal

Love. My Holy Spirit will take the innocent and make a pact of Love and Peace with them, to become fit and become His partner. My Holy Spirit will lift them and carry them - like a bridegroom carrying his bride across the threshold, He too will carry them behind the walls of the sanctuary where lie fathomless riches and mysteries, mysteries that no eye had seen before; and like a Spouse adorning His Bride with jewels He too will adorn them with imperial knowledge to delight in throne and sceptre. O what will My Holy Spirit not do for you!

My Holy Spirit is the zest of your life, the Royal Crown of Splendour, the Diadem of Beauty from My Mouth, the radiant Glory of the Living One, the Secret Revelation of your creation. My Holy Spirit is the flavour of your homilies in My Assemblies and the fulfilment of your Times... He is the Flaming Fire of your heart and the perception of My Mysteries; My Holy Spirit is the theme of your praises to Me revealing to your heart that I Am Who I Am, revealing to your spirit that I am your

Abba

and that you are My offspring, and My seed... Blessed be the pure in heart - they shall see Me. Rejoice and be glad and open up to receive My Holy Spirit so that you too may delight and hear My Voice! Open your hearts and you shall see My Glory, and like a child needing comfort, My Holy Spirit will comfort you whose love for you surpasses any human love. ♥

I, the Creator of the heavens and earth tell you, My Holy Spirit is the Spouse of the Bride, of She who held the Infant Who was to save you and redeem you, and in Whom through His Blood you would gain freedom and forgiveness of your sins. He is the Spouse of the One Whom He found like a garden enclosed, holding the rarest essences of virtues, a sealed fountain, the loveliest of Women, bathed in purity because of her unique perfection. My Spirit came upon Her and covered Her with His shadow and glorified Me making Her the Mother of God, the Mother of all humanity and the Queen of Heaven.[1] Such is the Richness of My Holy Spirit...

I am showering on all of you My Holy Spirit, now... today... I, Yahweh, the Almighty am telling you: I am giving you all this free gift to save you out of the greatness of the Love I have for you. Love and Loyalty now descend, I Yahweh lean down from heaven to embrace all of you; My saving help is offered from above to you - are you willing to comply with My given Law? Are you willing to entrust Me with your soul? Do not say I am unmoved by your misery and

---

[1] I want to note that when the Father was dictating to me this passage concerning Our Blessed Mother, if He were not God, I would have said He was exalted, so much was His Joy.

unresponsive to your prayers - if the flames lick up your countries and fires devour your people and if the inhabitants of the earth taste the disgrace of death it is all due to your great apostasy. You have shunned from My Holy Spirit - He who would have clothed you in blessings; He who would have made your heart and flesh leap and sing for joy to Me your God, but you preferred to become homeless, beggared and fatherless and today dwindling away in the shadows of death. How I pity you... O generation! How much longer can you defy Me? My Love fills the earth, My calls fill the mouths of My envoys and though My grief is acute and My Justice is now brimming over I can still relent and I can accept the homage you would offer Me. I am ready to forgive you through the Blood shed by My Son and through His Sacrifice if you take My Words to heart. ♥ Soon, very soon now, My Holy Spirit will blow on you with such force making a mighty sound ring out at the four corners of the earth, as a reminder before all the inhabitants of the earth. Then immediately at the sound of My Holy Spirit's Breath, the people of the earth all together would fall on their face to the ground in adoration of Me the Lord, the Almighty, the Most High, and in the end the people would bow low before the Throne of the Lamb and receive the Blessing from the Throne ♥ and now, I who created you and I who formed you, ask you: will I deign to hear your cry of repentance?

LOVE ME AND CONSOLE THIS HEART
SO UNLOVED AND SO UTTERLY MISUNDERSTOOD!
I HAVE MADE YOU A THREAT TO MY ENEMIES

October 6th, 1992

Lord, when Your words come to me, I devoured them. You have given me this celestial Manna to keep me alive and every Word You utter is my delight and the saving evidence of Your Love. Your Word is the joy of my soul, the cup of my consolation and the ravishments of my heart.

The world has inherited nothing but Deceptiveness, but Your Word from Your Mouth disinherited the world and all that is within it. Remember how I stood in Your Presence unlawful and naked? and yet instead of decreeing a disaster for my appalling and despicable behaviour, Your utterance pierced these layers of thick dark clouds, and as a king conquering a city, You conquered me placing Your glorious Throne in me. In the parched places of my wilderness You sprang Your Fountain of living Water, showing me Your favour and that from thereon I will be allowed to walk with I AM.

Yes daughter, I have never commanded you to sin - realize who is speaking to you and in whose presence you are in! I showed you and to all of you My Heart; I am coming to uproot what the world has sown: deceit after deceit, a harvest of Falsehood! Death is creeping below your doors and making its way in silence into your room,[1] making out of those dearly loved by Me, <u>corpses</u>, winnowing like sheaves left by the reaper, with no one to gather them. ♥

My Body is scourged daily from the sins of the world and, My little bearer, your Lord, who speaks to you now, tells you: I thirst for love. ♥ *Love Me and console this Heart so unloved and so utterly misunderstood! Pray for the sinners...*

Lord, our Shepherd, come and gather Your lambs one by one in Your Arms, holding them near Your Sacred Heart. All flesh is weak my Lord, and You know it, yet, among them there is a list of good men.....

Vassula, no man is good but God...

Then there is a list of generous souls whose good works should not be forgotten. I know that no one can glorify You as You deserve, but in our weakness and for the sake of Your Love, will you not hurry up Your Return, O Great One, and renew the walls of Your Sanctuary?

You shall be rebuilt![2]

Child, so favoured by Me, I have made you a threat to My enemies - these planters have done their planting and they will gather and eat their own fruit...[3] speak!

Ah, Lord, You have made the heavens and the earth with joy and with great power. You have created us with happiness and loved us with an everlasting love. Let even Your enemies yearn for Your Tenderness. Shine in each heart and turn EVERY heart of stone to You...

I shall pour out My Spirit on these too, My Vassula. The rebel shall turn into a devout servant, eager to serve Me, eager to worship Me. I shall display My Holiness in every heart and I shall feed them too with My sweet Manna. ♥ *Come, live holy for I am Holy. We, us?*
Yes, my Lord. We, us.

---

[1] I understood that room, means soul.
[2] God, with great majesty uttered these words.
[3] I had hesitated, and He stopped.

OUR TWO HEARTS ARE FILLED
WITH OVERWHELMING JOY
WHEN WE SEE YOU COMING TO US TO PRAY

October 8th, 1992

My Vassula, I am your Mother. 'Pethi-mou'[1] remember you are in Our Hearts - live for Jesus and He will give you an eloquence of speech to glorify Him. Your suffering leads you to sanctification and I tell you, in all Our grief a ray of consolation penetrates Our Two Hearts and We are filled with overwhelming joy when We see you coming to Us to pray. Learn that prayer, love and humility are the strongest weapons against Satan. Everyone of you makes part of the renovating process of the Church, but Satan in his fury will toss each one of you against each other if he finds you sleeping. Our Plan is to plant you all together in love and rebuild the Church on Love. You have now seen a dim reflection of how Satan works. I bless you and all those who contribute in this work. Pray My Vassula, and although the battle is in its full force, do not fear. I am near you.

YOU ARE MY GIFT TO ALL
TODAY I NEED ONE THING:
A HEART TO HEART CONVERSATION

October 9th, 1992

Vassula, listen and write: the devil and his angels are determined to expand their pernicious designs and make of the good things I am sending you venomous alleys. I look to the earth with grief because many ignore the lessons I have been giving you and death is penetrating in many houses, yet, many refuse to understand that evil draws evil. ♥ *The world, My child, in its apostasy is self-destructing itself...*

Lord?

I Am. Yes, confide to Me, unburden your heart and tell Me. I am listening.

---

[1]Greek for: my child.

Why would that monk want to prevent me from coming to You in this way? I am happy to be in this way with You. You and I, alone - after all it is Your Gift to me...

Yes, it is My Gift to you and <u>you</u> are My Gift to all. I once said to Martha:

> *"Martha! You worry and fret about so many things and yet few are needed, indeed only one; and it is Mary who has chosen the better part - it is not to be taken from her."*

and so I am telling him or anyone who comes your way to forbid you from coming to My Feet, like now, to listen to Me, write and be permanently together.

> *"You worry and fret over many things <u>I do not need</u>! Indeed, today I only need one thing:*
>
>> *a heart to heart conversation*
>> *a prayer without ceasing in adoration at My Feet*
>
> *<u>unite your heart to Mine</u> - this <u>is</u> the better part..."*

and you, My daughter, rejoice! For I have given you freely this Gift - it is not to be taken from you. ♥

October 11th, 1992
Famalicão - Portugal

Message for Padre Joakim Milleihro, the translator and publisher in Portugese of, 'True Life in God.'

Every word he translates caresses My Heart so lacerated, and every step they[1] take, glorifies Me, I the Lord bless them and their work. I Am is with them.

---

[1] The nuns helping Padre Joakim to publish 'True Life in God.'

October 12th, 1992
Fatima - Portugal

Peace be with you. Carry My Cross till the end, pray and meditate. Enliven My Church. ΙΧθΥΣ ⋙

October 14th, 1992
Fatima - Portugal

Vassula of My Sacred Heart, in the end every heart will learn the word 'reconciliation' and will accept one another in the heart; unity will be in the heart. ΙΧθΥΣ ⋙

IN THE END OUR TWO HEARTS SHALL TRIUMPH

October 15th, 1992

Our Blessed Mother speaks:

(I had joined the Pilgrims that were going to Poland, Czechoslovakia, Russia and Rome.)

Peace be with you. My Vassula, remember, I am leading this pilgrimage - all I ask from you is to listen to Jesus. All that comes your way, let it come; allow Jesus to work and speak through you. Little one, you have not yet understood how much Jesus loves you - bless Him. My Heart truly is united to His and in the end, Our Two Hearts shall triumph. We, us?

Yes! Glory be to God!

October 16th, 1992
Russia - Moscow

Lord, Almighty, blessed be Your Name. Now, this very day, Your Word is being accomplished. In 1987, You said ' go to your sister, Russia' - here I am, at her feet. You said, 'love her as I love her' - I am here to love her and if You want me to serve her, I will do it. Just utter Your command.

♥ *[1].... treasure what I have said to you; realize that My Plan for Russia is great; realize that I will use you for My Glory. My child have My Peace - with you I Am.*

SEE HOW MY PASSION FOR MANKIND REDUCED ME TO?

October 18th, 1992
Russia - Moscow

Shepherd of humanity, overthrow all kingdoms that do not call on Your Name!

Shepherd, You who lead us with loving care back into the Fold, Your anxious glances do not escape me, the swifter sound of Your Heart-beats have left in my own heart traces of sorrow. No, Lord, my ears are not deaf to Your secret sighs of grief, leaving my own breath weak. Shepherd, the eyes of my soul are witnessing today something never seen before; no, do not hold Your Head sideways - it is of no use hiding Your distress from me. You have set me too close to Your Heart not to notice Your movements... and the Branch of the Vine absorbed the sap <u>from</u> the Vine...

Beneath My skin I have placed you.[2] The heavens will wear away before My creation wakes... See how My Passion for mankind reduced Me to?

---

[1] Here the Lord gave me His order, but it should not be known to the others and to no one yet.
[2] Expression that means that I am in God.

Can I be of any use to You, my Shepherd?

You will pray, you will fast for My Sake and your footsteps should follow close to Mine. Pray that the Father's Hand does not fall at an hour when dreams muster the mind of this generation.

My Lord, my spirit absorbs Your grief. Come I beg You, let my heart and those hearts that love You comfort You and soothe Your pain. The eyes that once saw Your sorrow will never stay dry. Were You to pass me, I still should see Your movement and detect Your pain. I am only Your creature but You have placed me beneath Your skin, without any merits and for no reason. You fostered me. What shall I say then, when You, my God, stand up in front of me, the supreme God, so offended and so grieved? See? I am beneath Your skin, and yet, a mere creature, fashioned out of clay. Have I deserved the warmth of Your Body and Blood, the warmth of Your Heart and Your closeness? No...

Do you look forward to your dwelling in heaven, near Me, and making your way in the Light? Does your heart long for your permanent home?

Yes! Holy One! Oh yes!

♥ *My priest... you will enter My Court at the accomplishment of your mission. Although My Heart longs to take you into the heights of My Sanctuary, I could not take you prematurely - I still have more to say. My beloved, we shall pass the lanes and the street-corners together gathering the dead; you will draw them near Me and I will breathe in them. Little by little, therefore, I will wake up the dead so that your Shepherd's sobs cease...*

O may Your Words find fulfilment!

Rise then, spread My Message like a panoply around the world. I am with you, and you shall follow My vigorous stride; work promptly and do not worry - Satan can tear himself to pieces if he wills but you, for all his rage, will not be silenced or scathed - you will finish your race with Me. ♥

I HAVE ALREADY TAKEN ONE STEP IN HER, (RUSSIA)

October 18th, 1992
Moscow - Russia

Little one, have My Peace - let nothing take away this Peace I have given you. Realize how great is My Plan - I have great events yet to come; this country will honour Me more than any other country:

I have already taken one step in her...

Vassula, I will ask you to preach to My children of Russia - this will come to you, as I have taught you.[1] Be wise and proceed as I will indicate to you; remain nothing and I shall augment. My Heart is your home. ♥ I Am. IXθΥΣ ⤳

PROPHECY

RUSSIA WILL GOVERN THE REST OF MY CHILDREN IN HOLINESS

October 20th, 1992
Moscow - Russia

Russia will honour You in her poverty. Perhaps UNITY will come through her. Since You say that she will be the one who will glorify You most. Weren't these Your Sighs of Your sacerdotal prayer to the Father?

Come, write: My Peace I give you;
I am the Resurrection,

and resurrection shall soon take place in My daughter Russia. Do not be judge of her sons and daughters so that I will not be compelled to judge you. ♥ Were anyone perfect among you, you would still count for nothing in My Perfection. Soon the Glory will be given to Me in its fullness and Russia will govern the rest of My children in holiness.

---

[1]Meaning the Lord will bring things to my doorstep.

I, the Lord, am asking you for your prayers, your sacrifices and expiations so that all these things may lead My Russia near Me. In her wretchedness I will show My Mercy; in her weakness, My Power and My Authority; in her nothingness

all that I Am;

and in her aridity I shall make Rivers flow out of her. I shall uproot in her all that is not Me and in these empty spaces, plant My Graces in her - I shall plant seeds of Love and Peace. ♥

> *"Russia, it is not long ago since you broke your alliance with Me, burst your bonds and said: 'I will not serve You!' Now I shall give you children who will proclaim My Name in Holiness and say: 'blessed is He who restored our sight and touched our heart; blessed is He who changed our ways healing us.' Then, with Me in you and you in Me,*

you will live ♥

> *and with Our Two Hearts in your heart you will give Me the Glory foretold."*

Vassula, My bride, for My sake, pray for the full conversion of Russia. I, the Lord, bless you My child. Never forget that I am He who loves you most - My Heart can be touched... ΙΧθΥΣ ✕⊂▷

Later on that evening I was invited with a friend by a Russian Orthodox priest who works for Unity to assist a meeting on Tradition. The lady president said that anyone who wants to speak from the audience, will have eight minutes.

The Russian Orthodox priest asked the president on a piece of paper which was passed on to her, whether I could speak to the crowd too. I presume she knew who I was because she sent back a note saying 'no.'

The priest again wrote a second note, sent it to her, and her reply was once more negative. It was becoming a matter now for the angels to intervene. I called my angel, and asked him to gather the other angels who surround me to go and speak to her angel and make her change her mind.

Just then I felt Jesus intervening, as though He was asking Me: "what are you doing!?" "I am sending my angels..." He said: "I have told you before sending you to Russia that you were going to go only as a pilgrim, this time!" I suddenly remembered. But I said like a spoilt child: "O Lord! Please, I will not make a

70

discourse; just give me <u>three</u> minutes, just to introduce Your Message, nothing more. It is such an occasion Lord!" Hardly had I finished my words when the president suddenly sent another note allowing me eight minutes of speech. But the Good Lord nevertheless, gave me ten whole minutes...

TO YOU IN TURN MY CUP I WILL PASS

October 21st, 1992

Vassula, write:[1] "... and every tree of the field will learn that I, Yahweh, am the one who stunts tall trees and makes the low ones grow, who withers green trees and makes the withered green. I, Yahweh, have spoken and I will do it. ♥ "

Daughter, every time anyone wounds you, My Heart - an Abyss of Love - opens wide for you to absorb you in its depths. I repay every one of your wounds with Tenderness and Kisses from My Mouth... Daughter, are you willing to accept the crosses I am giving you?

.... I have asked you a question ....

Suffering has become my daily bread, but what an honour to share it with You. You come daily into my room to share my meal, side by side with me. You sup with me sharing my daily bread. You are my Sacrificer; pitilessly You bend Your bow aiming at me and You arrows are raining on the Target You have chosen. You make my soul leap like on fire, from Your arrows. And yet, when I do not have this bread, I ask: 'where is the bread that burns up one's heart?'

♥ My generosity and My kindness are not yet exhausted; the favours I have favoured you with will be renewed, for My Burning Love will consume you to ashes and I will make your soul drunk, to thirst for My arrows - you shall not be deprived... So rejoice and exult, for to you in turn My Cup I will pass... I mean to bring nation after nation to live under My shadow, and believe that the Father sent Me[2] Yes, the Day will come when all the earthly rulers, the governors and the commanders, the rich people and the men of influence, the whole population[3] will recognize Me as the Christ, Son of the Living God; and from every place, men will lift their hands up reverently in prayer and worship, all in one voice and heart;

---

[1] The Lord asked me to write from Ez 17:24.
[2] John: 17:21.
[3] Apocalypse 6:15.

for this I need victim souls, for this I need collaborators - so do not fear men. My Eyes watch over you. If one person loves anointing My Name and others lack charity, challenging Me, to which one will the Master offer His heritage? My daughter, be in peace. I resent those who testify My Word yet scoff and mock Me in others - let them make their peace with Me.

And you, My daughter, do not wriggle in My Hands - allow Me to sweep away the particles hindering My passage in your soul, let Me proceed without your objecting. You do not need reminders with engraved inscriptions, I want My passage free. I have as you said, favoured you, to hear My Voice; I have allowed your soul to stretch out and touch Me - what have you felt? What did your fingertips feel around My Heart? Petals of roses? No? Then what did you feel? Different bouquets of chosen flowers? Oh no, those who receive bouquets of flowers are loved; then what did your hands feel? Thorns? Yes, and much more than a crown of thorns - you have felt the lance's blade... I want you to expiate for all those who offend Me and wound Me. I am determined to perfect you by aiming My arrows on you, by bowing you and making you obedient and humble. Your soul will learn to endure the ordeal of being openly and publicly calumniated and ridiculed; since you are unable to deign to bow low, My intervention then is necessary - I would not want you to appear to Me in the last minute unacceptable. My very core is yearning for your perfection so do not ever complain about those who calumniate you in written form and in public. Your sufferings glorify Me so let your soul thirst for such offenses made upon you - what greater gift could I offer a soul who still is so far from perfection? Come close to Me and rely on My pardon. ♥
ΙΧθΥΣ ⋙

YAHWEH ASKS THEM TO SEEK HIS FACE NOW AND THEN

October 21st, 1992

This message was for (...). The Father spoke.

Look, presents and gifts I do not receive many - the offering and the generosity of him whom I have chosen to counsel you pleases Me. Beg Me to guide your steps into this task so that you may proceed into the truth - I find My delight when you hear Me. Speak of My instructions before My children - tell them that Yahweh, your Eternal Father, Father of all, asks them to seek His Face now and then...

72

Yahweh continues:

Praise Me Vassula, pray and be concerned only for My Interests. I Yahweh bless you from the core of My Heart - I love you!

PROPHECY

I WILL LIFT HER (RUSSIA) TO BECOME
THE HEAD OF MANY NATIONS

October 25th, 1992
Rome

Altar! I will place on you My Words. ♥ Hear and write: you are under My Tent, so abandon yourself each day to Me that I may do My Will in you; be placid and willing - you are very precious to Me, My child. Vassula, My dove, Wisdom who has been up to now your Educator will continue to teach you and tell you what your duties are. I will appeal from you love for your sister Russia, I will send you back to her and with you My Own Heart. ♥ Russia is especially dear to Me; indeed today Russia is like an open field ready to be sown; her soil is ready to receive any seed. I have given revelations through My Spirit to be sown in her - nobody will be allowed to lay down any other foundation than My very Own foundation. It is I, God, who designed Russia for My Glory and it is through her that light will shine out of her darkness, it is through her light that your generation's heart will be enlightened with the knowledge of My Glory. I shall pour out My Spirit on the House that I had given her and I will display My Holiness in her to honour My Name. It was of her that I spoke in the past through My little prophets; I tell you, all her splendour she once had I will give in double, for she will put her whole heart into following Me and seek My Holy Face once more. ♥ No one will gloat over her for I will lift her to become the head[1] of many nations. ♥ In her poverty I will rebuild My Kingdom, ah Vassula! Just wait and see!

CONTRADICTED AND DISBELIEVED FROM WITHIN
MY HOUSE YOU WILL BE
PERSECUTION WILL BE YOUR DAILY BREAD

November 1st, 1992

Zeal for You devours me, I am Yours Lord. Turn to me please and fill my mouth to revive me. Rescue me from human tongue...

Accept the homage that I offered you now.[1]

I love You Lord to madness.

Love Me for those who do not. I Am is watching over you. Little by little I have raised you, dearest soul, that you may glorify Me; you are to teach this generation the words: Love and Unity. Listen Vassula of My Sacred Heart, My Love will save you. Puny and despised you will be, contradicted and disbelieved from within My House you will be, persecution will be your daily bread - these will be your compensations on earth, for all these things will direct your steps into My Kingdom. Your traces left behind will bring many other souls to Me, therefore, concentrate on My Own traces and follow Me. ♥ I am glad you confided this revelation to My Mother, I tell you, you could not have chosen better. My Mother will be your defender - no one will be able to damage these writings; I have blessed them ♥ so dear to Me. I love you, never doubt of My Love. I Jesus am with you, I delight in you. ♥ ΙΧθΥΣ ⤙⊃

BLEMISHES IN YOUR SOUL SADDEN ME
AND ARE A HORROR TO ME

November 5th, 1992

Peace My little one - raised by Me, enter into My Sacred Heart. You will overcome your oppressors, yes every single one will fall.

I am weak and far from being strong...

---

[1] I just heard how someone I know is persecuting me.

Keep in your mind that I Am is the Rock and your strength will come from this Rock - altar? I will look after you - you must leave Me free to purify you; blemishes in your soul sadden Me and are a horror to Me. My altar I want without blemish, I want pure; I want to clothe you in splendid robes. Bless Me, I who am your counsellor.

I bless You Lord Jesus.

I need to plunder you and make you poor - I love poverty. Earthborn, have you nothing to tell Me?

I am Your victim and it is with You and into Your Hands I want to be, to be able to feel what You felt when on earth. I want to taste You.

I will grant you to taste Me if this is what you sigh for... I will, if you allow Me, subdue you to My Will... and you will learn how great is My Name and how perfect is the One who made you these advances... IXθYΣ ⤳⟨◻⟩

SACRIFICE
IF THE WORLD HATES YOU, IT IS BECAUSE YOU LOVE ME
PRAY FOR THOSE WHO PLOT INCREDIBLE SCHEMES
AGAINST MY HOLY SPIRIT

November 10th, 1992

Peace be with you. ♥ *Today's lands have been totally polluted and have everything but Me - what seems right to the world is abhorrent in My Sight and is already condemned by Me. If the world hates you it is because you love Me; let your testimony be valid in My Eyes and I tell you, your testimony will only be valid were you to sacrifice entirely for the salvation of souls and show your love by laying down your life for your friends and for those you call your enemies, so that when My Day comes you need feel no shame. I, Myself, will provide you with My Strength - in the meantime carry on the work I have given you and shout for joy, rejoice because with My Power I will break through their wall and let everything that had been hidden from you to be exposed to light. Your eyes will see crawling before you all sorts of animals and snakes, but do not be afraid of those who kill the body, I tell you they cannot kill the soul. Fear him rather who can destroy both body and soul in hell! Follow in My Footprints and do not look for honour or praise - if the world takes you for imposters know that you are genuine, for the first imposter the world took was Me. Love! and forgive! Pray for those who plot incredible schemes against My Holy Spirit and do not judge them lest what is fatal for them, turns to be fatal on you. Let Me correct them; let everything you do be planted in love. I shall provide you and fill you with consolations. Every thorn in My Body will be removed in the end. Love will triumph.*

I LOVE YOU TO TEARS

November 15th, 1992

> "If only my miseries could be weighed, and all my ills be put on the scales! But they outweigh the sands of the seas: what wonder then if my words are wild?"

Job 6:2-3

I shiver with horror to think I might be wrong! Will I be found with blame in Your Presence my God? Yet I have taken root in You, I saw You standing there, silent, with Your Hand outstretched as someone expecting alms. Then I heard a Voice, a Name was given me, and my soul succumbed into My Father's Arms. O God! How I love You!

My child, My child... How I the Lord love you! I love you to tears... cease listening to the evil one who tries to destroy all the good things I have given you; have faith in My Love, I will never fail you[1]... Never[2]... So have My Peace, this Peace I have given you, and know My child that greater love than Mine you will never meet... Ah, My child, cling on the hem of My robe; I am here and with you. ♥

---

[1] He said these words almost as a whisper.
[2] He whispered this word.

JOIN YOUR PRAYERS WITH THESE OF THE SAINTS

November 19th, 1992

Your auxiliary slave is at Your Service.

Vassula of My Sacred Heart, beloved of My Soul, come to Me. When persecuted enter My Sacred Heart and taste My Love. Among many, I have chosen you to follow Me into the Path that leads to Unity; I have made you My pupil and not only have I become your Educator and Teacher but I have become your Spouse - with Me you will lack nothing beloved.

Do You want me in dictation, Lord?

Every minute of your life! Every single minute of your life, be with Me! In prayer, in dictation, in meditation, in receiving Me in the Holy Eucharist, at the hours of adoration, prove your love to Me! Prove your thirst for Me, prove your faithfulness by remaining united in love with My Heart. ♥ Be steadfast, dependable on My Strength and always look forward to meeting Me. Ah, little one, have you not understood? Have you not noticed the greatness of the Love I have for you, and My friendship? ... And now, while you are still here, join your prayers with these of the saints and remember, I know perfectly well what you have in your heart; I know your needs - everything! You all belong to Me alike and would I not give My Life all over again for you were it needed![1]...

Here I am sending My Spirit to remind you of the greatness of My Love, and to ask you to withdraw from the world that has everything but Me - for each one of you I have a place in My Sacred Heart. Come, unite your heart with My Heart and live Our Messages. I bless each one of you, leaving the Sigh of My Love on your forehead - be one!

---

[1] These words were given with much expression since they came out of His Divine Heart.

A SHORT PRAYER TO THE FATHER

November 27th, 1992

Peace be with you. It is I, Jesus. Pray with me and say:

> *Father, all I ask from*
> *You now is to strengthen*
> *my faith. Amen.*

I repeated it with Jesus.

MY CHURCH IS DIVIDED

November 29th, 1992
Manila - Philippines

I am your good Shepherd - I heard your call from above so how could I resist your cry, when I hear laments and your agony? I have come in this way to speak to you and remind your hearts of My request[1]: have you all reconciled with your brothers, with your sisters, with everybody? Only a few have... here I am, sending you word again. I do not come as a Judge, not yet, and if I reproach you, it is because of the greatness of the love I have for you... I am a Jealous God and I want prayers, prayers without ceasing.

Ah, beloved children, if you knew how My Heart is lacerated every time one of you postpones for later on My desires... I tell you, I will soon descend in full force with My Holy Spirit to give sight to the blind and take away the sight from those who say they see...

The spirit who is hovering over this world is a rebellious spirit, ruling the world to live a Godless life, thus profaning My Sanctuary - are you not all of you My Sanctuary? Delight your Father in Heaven and pray for the Reconciliation of this world.

Happy the peacemakers when they work for Peace!, they will be called children of the Most High. Pray that My Church be one. Today there is a division in My

---

[1]In .... the Lord gave a message to the Philippines, asking them to reconcile.

78

Church as never before; like Cain and Abel, brothers, yet unlike one from the other; one blood, yet different; one was sincere, the other one not, one was well disposed, the other one was ill-disposed and displeasing Me. ♥ *One was faithful and devout, the other one treacherous and a rebel. These are today's members in My Church - I have two sorts: one, devout, the other one a rebel; My Church is divided.*

I tell you truly that My Kingdom is among you. My Holy Spirit today is blowing on you all to revive what little is left in you, and to bring the rebels back to their senses. My Holy Spirit of grace is blowing on you My Passionate Love; the sheep that belong to Me will recognize My Voice from far; soon, I shall make disciples shine out. I, your King am blessing each one of you from the core of My Heart. Be one! ΙΧθΥΣ ✂⊂▷

THE WORLD DOES NOT LISTEN TO OUR TWO HEARTS
LISTEN TO YOUR FATHER

November 29th, 1992

Our Blessed Mother gives a message to the Filippinos:

Like a Mother I come to ask you to listen to your Father; hear Him and do whatever He asks you to do. ♥ **I have shown you the Wounds of Our Hearts in a special way; I shall remain with you in this way for only a short time now but I shall not leave you, you who are the Shepherd's lambs, without making sure that you have shelter and pasture.** ♥

The world again misjudged the Times and cannot recognize the Signs either, the world does not listen to Our Two Hearts, nor understand Them - they are rejecting Us... but the hour is near when a Light will shine from above and Our Two Hearts, like Two Lamps shining near each other will revive this world, bringing it from darkness to light. Those Two Hearts the world combatted will prevail in the end! and the kingdoms of the world will pass away and will be replaced by My Son's Kingdom.. this is all very near you now! When you leave from here[1] leave with the Lord's peace and My peace. ♥

---

[1] The Church we were in.

I HAVE ESTABLISHED MY THRONE INSIDE YOUR HEART

December 1st, 1992

Your word is my delight, my Life and my hope. What have You found in my wicked heart to establish Your Throne inside it? Day and night You show Your favours to me.

I have established My Throne inside your heart to save you and to deliver you; I have established My Throne inside your heart to reign over you; I have established My Throne inside your heart to endow you with My Spirit - your poverty enchanted Me, your misery attracted Me. If such favour is shown to the wicked, will I not much more favour the righteous, oh men of little faith? I am the First and the Last, the Beginning and the end. ♥

A ☧ Ω

NEVER LET GO OF THE HEM OF MY CLOTHES

December 2nd, 1992
Australia

Show me the Light of Your Holy Face, raise my soul to the heights and let me see You!

Compensate Me then and evangelize with love for Love. Every word you will utter for the glory of My Holy Name, will be blessed so that like a dove it will flutter and reach where it will make its home. IC[1] Jesus ♥ *compensate Me and give Me your time, your mind, your hand and your heart to use for My Glory, then watch My Lips, touch My Heart and write - never let go of the hem of My clothes!* ♥

Just when Jesus signed and sealed this message, He said to me in a whisper: 'Sarajevo[2] shall perish.'

---

[1]"ic" are initials found on Greek icons where Jesus is portrayed. IC, is short for 'Jesus ICOUC.'
[2]Sarajevo is a town in ex-Yugoslavia. Three days after the Lord said this, on the 5th December, 1992, Sarajevo was attacked.

WE ARE PARTNERS ARE WE NOT?
AND THE POWER OF MY HOLY SPIRIT WILL LIFT YOU

December 3rd, 1992
Australia

Before my mission in Australia.

Look at Me! Receive the One who loves you most! My lamb, I am with you and My Word will be brought into your mouth and It shall cut and pierce their hearts; good and bad will hear you. You will preach and teach the knowledge I Myself have given you through these years. Perseverance? is that what you need child?

Yes, my Lord!

I will keep you company to revive your soul. My presence will encourage your heart and you will persevere - we are partners, are we not?

We are!

Then do not be afraid. I and you, you and I and the power of My Holy Spirit will lift you and will whisper and remind you the sound Teachings I have given you - do not fear, I have never failed you. I will give you an eloquence of speech to give honour to your King. ♥ ΙΧθΥΣ ⋈⊃

MY GLORY WILL BE SHARED WITH
THE INNOCENT SOULS

December 3rd, 1992
Australia

Christ, You are the theme of my praise in our assemblies. I have treasured the instructions You have given me from Your Lips. I invoke You now Sacred Heart to help me display the Fathomless Tenderness, the Love of the Almighty God, Our Father, the delicacy of Your Own Sacred Heart and the Infinite Riches of Your Spirit.

I tore the Heavens and came down into your room, so now join in the saints' choir and sing with your whole heart, yes, wholeheartedly. My glory will be shared with the innocent souls, the poor and those who united their hearts to Mine. I will display My Love and show everyone that greater love than Mine you will not meet. See what you have? Love Himself comes to your room to speak to you; you have seen Me face to face. I, Jesus, bless you from the core of My Heart - feel loved - I, Jesus Christ am resurrected and alive and __am__ near you, __now__ ... IC.

THIS APOSTASY BEGGARED YOU

December 7th, 1992

Just before the meeting, God, our Father gave me this message:

Write: tell them that I am the Most Tender Father - tell them how I lean to reach them, __now__.

Love and Loyalty now descend to embrace all of you, to renew you, to revive you and lift you up from the lethargy that covers this earth. Do not say I am too far to reach, unmoved by your misery and unresponsive to your calls. If the flames lick up your countries and fires devour the people of the earth it is all due to the great apostasy that seized nation after nation infiltrating in the heart of My Law. This apostasy beggared you and made you believe you are fatherless... how I pity you! O generation, for how long must I wait? My warnings and My calls echo the earth and though My grief is acute and My Justice now brimming over, I can still relent and I can accept the homage you would offer Me. I am ready to forgive you through the Blood shed by My Son and through His Sacrifice, if you take My Words to heart. I who created you out of Love ask you:

Will I hear from you your cry of repentance? ...

Daughter, glorify Me and reveal My Holy Face with love to everyone! I bless you and everyone accompanying you.

DEMONSTRATE THE CONVINCING POWER OF MY HOLY SPIRIT

December 9th, 1992
Australia

Peace be with you. Favoured by My Father, be My Echo! Establish My Kingdom in Australia, sow My seeds of Love everywhere and in all directions; do not delay, and answer to all requests given you. I will give you enough strength to promulgate My Message... Demonstrate the convincing power of My Spirit; demonstrate how My Spirit uplifts, instructs and reveals the depths of the Truth and of the Eternal God; demonstrate to the unlearned the reality of spiritual things given by the Spirit and uncover the Knowledge given by My Spirit; demonstrate the full power of My Spirit, how He develops, testifies and gratifies the poor, the simple, the humble, but shies away from the rich, the wise, the proud who assess My Spirit with their natural understanding and evaluate everything in terms of their spirit. ♥ *Vassula, evaluate your spiritual growth and do not doubt of My grace. I, Jesus, am your Teacher and Master - never doubt. Ic, have My Peace.*
ΙΧθΥΣ ⤜⟩

I WILL NEVER IMPOSE MYSELF ON YOU

December 10th, 1992
Adelaide - Australia

Before the meeting:

Feel happy that I have saved you. Allow Me now to use you for My glory. Bring My children to understand the Knowledge I have passed on to you. Carry on the way you proceeded in the other assemblies. Smile at Me, My Love for you is greater than you think! Come, by grace I lifted you and millions of others, allow Me now to guide your step, Ic. ♥

Jesus!

I Am.

Do not go yet!

Why? Do you wish Me to remain?[1] Ah, you see? I will never impose Myself on you...

Jesus?

I Am.

Speak to me please.

Love loves you; love Me and thirst for Me as I thirst for you. Caress Me now and then by allowing Me to speak in your heart. Understand, soul, that you are not meant for this world but My Own Kingdom in Heaven, so renounce all that holds you to the world and look for heavenly things. Come, we, us?

Yes Lord! **IXθYΣ** ⤝◠◗

DO YOU WANT TO PASS THIS ERA'S THRESHOLD BY BLAZING FIRE? WITH ALL YOUR HEART *HALLOW MY NAME*

December 13th, 1992

Our Father, who art in Heaven, hallowed be thy Name... Our Father, whose love is revealed to the least of us, have mercy on Your creation! You have given us as a free gift - our liberty - to use as we please, but we have turned our liberty against us. Like a razor-blade in an infant's hand, we use it, hacking ourselves to death... O come! and turn our attention to Your Holy Name, or we will slice ourselves to pieces! I invoke You God Almighty in our troubles, will You rescue us, or will You hide from my petition?

Daughter, you are in charge of My Message, and I have been sending you in the world from nation to nation to cry out repentance and reduce this wilderness - indeed, the crowds throng around you. It has come to their ear that I Am is speaking and nation after nation is talking about you, they say to each other: "let us go and hear what God is saying." They come in thousands and sit down in front of you and listen to your words, but who acts on them? As far as they are

---

[1] I could not answer Him. Jesus as a rule asked me to be with Him for half an hour before any meeting. Today I had come late. Time was pressing and I wanted to get ready too.

concerned, you are like a love song beautifully sung to music; your words enchant them, but who among them puts My Messages into practice? Have they understood the words: reconciliation, peace, love and unity?

When brimstone and devouring flames will take place, and they are very near you now, they will learn that I had sent a prophet among them.

From the beginning I had given you My Commandments, I had asked you to love Me, your Lord, with all your heart, with all your soul and with all your mind; today I am asking you to allow Me to touch your soul so that your heart will be able to praise Me and tell Me that neither death nor life, no angel, no prince, nothing that exists, nothing still to come, not any power, or height or depth, nor any created thing, will ever come between you and your love to Me. I am your Stronghold - know that My Love is revealed even to the very least of you. Do not search your salvation in the light of the world, since you know that the world cannot give you Life.

Soon My Throne and of the Lamb will be in its place and your soul will be renewed with My Transcendent Light, because I, your Father, intend to restore the memory of your soul and make your heart sing to Me the word Abba - Father! I tell you, you do not belong to the world, so why do you still allow yourselves to be deceived over and over again?

Since the foundations of the earth I have called you by your name but when I proposed Peace, universal Peace, nearly all of you were for war, yet I am pouring out My Holy Spirit now to remind you of your true foundations and that all of you are My seed - but today My seed is filled up with dead words... I am the Holy One who held you first - for how long will your soul resist Those Eyes who saw you first? and for how long will your soul deny My distressed calls? Many of you are still fondling the Abomination of the Desolation in the most profound domain of your soul. Can you not see how the Viper repeatedly is deceiving you in the same way he deceived Adam and Eve? Satan is suggesting to you, untiringly and subtly to cut off all your heavenly bonds that bond you to Me, <u>your Father in heaven</u>; he mesmerized the memory of your soul to make you believe you are fatherless thus creating a gulf between you and Me, your God. Satan wants to separate you from Me and cut off your umbilical cord that unites you to Me in which Rivers of Life flow into you. ♥

Generation, you have still not set your minds for Me - when will you decide to return to Me? Do you want to pass this era's threshold by blazing fire, by brimstone and devouring flame? How could your soul trade My Glory for a worthless imitation that the evil one offers you daily. Ask Me for <u>your daily bread</u> and I shall give it to you! Why are you all so willing to listen to the Viper? You and I know that Satan is the father of lies, then why are you still listening to him?

I, your Creator, am your Father and I am calling you back to Me; believe in My distressed calls. Will your soul continue to befriend the Rebel, or will you deign to come down from your throne and repent? It is for you to decide - there is not much time left.

I am reminding you to beware of the false teachers and the false prophets who induce in your soul desolation and misinterpret the gospels, telling you that the Holy Spirit is not with you to remind you of your foundations nor of where you come from. They have already made a desolation out of your soul and dug a vast gulf between you and Me your Father - do not let them expand this desolation in your soul and mislead you into believing I have left you orphans. These false prophets have made out of My Son Jesus, a liar and out of the gospels an echoing cymbal, empty with emptiness. They made out of My Word a gaping grave - so beware of those false teachers, who tell you that My Holy Spirit cannot descend to perform in you miracles and wonders. Beware of them who condemn My Holy Spirit, who in your days more than anytime, reminds you of your foundations. Beware of them who keep up the outward appearance of religion but reject the inner power of it, the inner power that is My Holy Spirit.

And if anyone of you is calumniated and dejected because you are witnessing the Truth, turn to your Holy Mother - she will console your soul and provide you with courage. If the world inflicts on you impressive wounds, turn to your Mother and she will dress your wounds with her Maternal Love and Affection. Like She took care of My Beloved Son, your Holy Mother will take care of you too. In your misery and distress she comes flying to you and takes you into Her Heart, that same Heart who conceived your Saviour. Your Holy Mother in Heaven will teach you to enlarge My Kingdom on earth by teaching you to love Me - so let love be the principle of your life; let love be your root. Allow Me, your Father, to bond you to Me; allow Me to touch your soul. Come to Me and thrust yourself into My Arms. What greater bliss than being held by those Hands that created you? Place your ear on My Mouth, this Mouth that breathed in you through your nostrils: <u>Life</u>, and from the dust of the soil I revived you to conquer the earth; I touched you and asked you to listen to My Word since then. Come, you must set your heart right, renounce the iniquities that stain your soul and with all your heart

HALLOW MY NAME

PRAY WITH ME TO THE FATHER
(*PRAYER IS GIVEN*)

December 17th, 1992

Lord, Father and Educator of my life, who disciplined my heart, You who ravished my soul with a single one of Your glances, do not hide Your Holy Face from me; return that I may contemplate on You. O Jesus, come! Come to us where light itself is like the dead of night!

Your King is here... Pray with Me to the Father:

Father
I consecrate myself
in soul and body to Your service,
so that Your Eyes and Your Heart
never leave me.
Set Your Royal Throne inside me
and give me Your orders,
make me advance in purity of heart
to accomplish
all that You have given me.
Amen. ♥

Daughter, I will complete this journey with you. Do not be afraid. For your part, if you walk with Me at My pace, you shall not lack. If you turn away from Me, I will double your crosses to save you...[1] *Whoever returns to Me, I shall not turn him away. Listen to My Heart-beats so that their sound spare you any thought of rebellion. I, Jesus, bless you.* ΙΧθΥΣ ⤳⃝

---

[1] I understood that if I will not follow Him, He will also leave me and with crosses only. Seeing that I misunderstood Him, He added the following sentence.

WHEN WILL THEY PASS A DECREE
BY UNANIMOUS VOTE TO CELEBRATE
THE FEAST OF EASTER ALL IN ONE DATE?

December 21st, 1992

Read in unity week in Los Angeles and Sacramento:

Daughter of My Sacred Heart, I would like you to write: hear from heaven My Voice. ♥ *My Words of <u>Reconciliation</u>, <u>Peace</u> and <u>Unity</u> have not been heard nor have they been respected. I have spoken once and I will not speak again; I will add nothing now.*

Lord, it is not easy apparently.[1]

<u>I want your voice to thunder this time in January!</u>[2] I want your voice to thunder as loud as ever! You will speak on My behalf. Let the whole world hear - the days are now counted, there is not much time left and grace that enfolded mankind shall come abruptly and all of a sudden at its end... this will be done so that the world realizes how great was My Mercy and My Goodness that had flowed down from above year after year....

Tell those who work for unity to look up at the skies - see how far they are from the earth? This is how far their hearts are from one another, this is how far they are apart.[3] ♥ *<u>When will they all pass a decree by unanimous vote to celebrate the feast of Easter all in one date</u>? I am weary of hearing their noble language, perhaps it is suitable and eloquent for them but to Me it sounds like a stroke on a gong because it is empty with emptiness. I have come to talk to them - first, out of concern, then out of pity, but no one yet to this day has lowered his voice to hear My Voice. Alas for you, who say you are at My service yet prevent My Kingdom from finding unity and stability! But it is not you who will bring My Kingdom together... For you do not understand anything and never will... If you, in spite of My heavenly calls, did not sound the depths of My Heart, how would you unravel the arguments of My Mind, how can you fathom the Riches of My Sacred Heart? I have not spoken in parables, nor have I spoken in riddles, I have taken plain words to speak to you. I reprimanded the officials and I collected them together to talk to them[4] but have they observed the prompting of My Heart?*

---

[1] I wanted to say: 'to unify the dates of Easter.' This is what those working for unity had told me. But Jesus cut me and continued, with power in His Voice.
[2] Month of Unity.
[3] Jesus here seems to direct their step suggesting what they would have to do.
[4] Using me as His Mouthpiece.

Their duty was to make an official appeal. I reprimanded the authorities[1] I had not come that day[2] to attack them, but to offer them oil to fill up their lamps, lest further harm be done to My Church. How many of them stretched out their hands to heaven, calling Me? Do they realize how, twice[3] My Blood is shed like water? May My groans reach their ears this time...

What My right Hand planted has been severed in two, then in three, then hacked - where is the entire vine[4] I had planted? ...There was once a vine; every season I expected it to yield grapes; it covered valleys, mountains and extended beyond the seas, because it had taken root in My own property, in My own inheritance. I had spread its branches to reach to the four corners of the earth and fill the world with fruit, but instead of keeping it they neglected it, allowing thorns and briars to multiply around it, choking branch after branch, shoot after shoot. That chosen plant My right Hand had planted has been levelled now to the ground and the beauty and glory and the fruit it gave have now fallen down like rotten fruit. There is not need then to swell with pride and cease to have proud eyes in case your errors multiply and your deeds recoil on your own head. I have come to fill your lamp with oil, light your lamp and use it now so that you see where you are going - whosoever neglects to light his lamp this time and use it, it will be taken away from him and given to someone else. Let them pray and say these words:

O Lord, You who stand among us,
shepherd us.
Set Your Royal Throne in
the middle of Your vine
and give us Your orders.
O Holy Lord of all holiness
purify us
so that we preserve the integrity
of Your House and Your vine.
Lovingly intervene and protect
what Your right Hand cultivated.
We have failed You
but we know,
we believe,
and we trust,
that You will open wide Your
Gateway
to let the River of Life flow

---

[1] At the World Council of Churches.
[2] Using me as His Mouthpiece.
[3] The two Easters: Roman Catholic and Orthodox.
[4] Could be interpreted as Church, or God's people.

on Your vine;
and once more from it will
sprout branches that will
bear fruit and become a royal vine,
more kingly than ever before, because
Your Holy Spirit
the giver of Life
will overshadow it. ♥ *Amen.*

and you, My Vassula, your sufferings will teach you to be patient. Have you not heard that patience brings perseverance and perseverance brings hope? and this hope, upon this hope will raise My Kingdom. Let every part of yourself now glorify Me.

My Holy Spirit marked you with My Seal, so do not be afraid. Pastors, priests, teachers, bishops and cardinals will recognize the Shepherd's Call and I will renew their mind so that their old self is crushed and they will fully realize that I am on My way back to transfigure the whole of My creation in the goodness and holiness of the

Truth.

Come, My daughter, My precious one, I Am is with you. ♥

AS FOR YOUR NATION I WILL MELT IT DOWN
AS ONE MELTS IRON - WITH FIRE

January 6th, 1993

Jesus? Beloved One of the Father, my country's[1] fields are ravaged[2], they have now become the haunt of the lizard and the spider - are You no longer there? Are You no longer in this nation? Why does it make no progress? Why are You leaving them far behind? Death has creeped in under their doors... Son of the Almighty

---

[1] Greece.
[2] Spiritually.

God, when will You display Your Holiness in this nation? ..."Vassilia mou, yiati kles?"[1]

I weep on her excessive pride... How am I to deal with their excessive pride? They do not listen to My Spirit and are following the dictates of their own proud hearts.

Truthfully, Lord of all Holiness, am I not doing my best to serve You, am I not interceding for Unity? Can I bend iron with my bare hands?[2] Your Fire though can do it. Your wealth and Your Treasures of Your Sacred Heart can do it.

Then I will have to ask more from you... I will have to ask more from you. All that you give Me will be to bind you all together in love, and enlighten your hearts so that your spirit may open to My Spirit who will teach you the depths of your Father in Heaven, and the hidden jewels of Wisdom. ♥

Poverty is at Your Feet, to serve You Almighty One.

Yes! Trust Me. I will always uphold you, so do not fear... Look at Me... My palate is dryer than parchment and the Father will not bear this sight much longer; the world is offending Him and His whole Kingdom. ♥ *The world has become so wicked and My Arm cannot much longer hold away His Arm from falling upon you...[3] Iron can be melted, so do not lose courage... do not forget that I have posted you with a sword in your hand, to flash like lightning. For the proud, these News I have given you to carry, displease mightily their heart. They trouble their spirit and cause their knees to tremble. As for your nation, I will melt it down as one melts iron - with Fire* ♥ *... and they will advance into holiness.*

THE SACRED HEART

Message to someone from the Sacred Heart:

Something[4] which has existed, can never die, Something which revives fervour and brings visible life in My Church will never extinct. You are witnessing the revival of My Sacred Heart with your own eyes, and of the One whom you say: "I know

---

[1]Greek: "My King, why do You weep?"
[2]The iron rods of my vision representing the three Christian Churches.
[3]Suddenly Our Lord stopped, and looked at me, as if He remembered something, then spoke.
[4]The Sacred Heart.

Him and I love Him." What is being carried out today does not go without suffering and sacrifice. I will keep alive the Devotion of My Sacred Heart and all that I have taught surroundering it - this is My Own promise. You have been given to witness the revival of My Sacred Heart so that you could give your testimony. To be the sacrifice of the One who takes your sins away is a privilege. I accept the testimony you are giving Me in My Spirit. So what you are seeing with your own eyes is the fulfilment of your times. ♥

IN THE END EVERYONE WILL WORSHIP ME

January 17th, 1993
Los Angeles - Eve of Unity Week

Lord, I pray as You have prayed: may we all be one, as the Father is in You and You in Him, so that the rest of the world may believe it was the Father who sent You. For this I pray too: for the sheep who are not of Your Fold, that they too will listen to Your Voice; I pray for the Moslems, the Jews and others that they may come to love You from today onwards. Amen.

I have heard you, I have heard you, My friend ♥ *- in the end everyone will worship Me.* IXθΥΣ ⤚◁▷

THAT THEY ALL MAY BE ONE

January 18th, 1993
Sacramento

Today is my birthday and the first day of Unity week. It was also once the Feast of Peter's Chair. Today I have been invited to speak at the Cathedral of the Blessed Sacrament by the very holy bishop Francis A Quinn. In the afternoon just before my meeting, the people who invited me offered me a present. When I saw it I felt that it came from Jesus. For He had said to me these words on the 21st October 1992: ..."rejoice and exult for <u>to you in turn My Cup I will pass</u>... I mean to bring nation after nation to live under My shadow, and believe that the Father sent Me. Yes, the Day will come when all the earthly rulers, the governors and the men of influence, the whole population, will recognize Me as the Christ, Son of the Living God; and

92

from every place, men will lift their hands up reverently in prayer and worship, all in one voice and heart..." and this is what they offered me: a gold-plated chalice. Engraved on it are these words:

> That they all may be one
> Feast of Christian Unity
> January 18 1993

Then the two bishops that were present celebrated mass after my talk. The choir sang in the cathedral and everything was majestic. They used my chalice during that mass for unity, consecrating the Precious Blood of Jesus inside it.

When I was giving my talk in the cathedral, and was looking at the crowds that had amassed - an estimated 1,800 people - I felt sad. There I was, sent by the Lord, to give a speech on Unity and facing perhaps 98% Roman Catholics; 'but of the men of my people[1] not one was with me' - there were even Moslems and Jews in the cathedral... But the Lord kept His surprise gift for my birthday till later on. Just before mass, in walks an Orthodox priest with his assistant. After mass he asked to talk to me. We met at the sacristy and I understood what the Lord was saying to Me: "Russia will be the country who will glorify Me most" - he was a Russian Orthodox priest... In the darkness of our division a tiny light of hope will shine of unity. This little light of hope is Russia. Unity will come through Russia and she will glorify God! I told the Russian priest that he was my birthday present from Jesus. His name is Fr. Vassili, which is the male name of my name, Vassula.

The other sign that unity will be brought by Russia was that when I asked the Lord to choose an opening prayer, He chose the prayer of a Russian priest: Fr. Sergius Bulgakov. He had asked me to open at random and I did, and my eyes saw first this prayer that I wrote on December 29th, 1989. Here it is again:

> O Jesus Christ, our Lord and
> Saviour, Thou didst promise
> to abide with us always.
> Thou dost call all Christians to
> draw near and partake of Thy
> Body and Blood. But our sin
> has divided us and we have
> no power to partake of
> Thy Holy Eucharist together.
> We confess this our sin and we pray Thee

[1] Greek Orthodox. (I heard that the Greek bishop had forbidden the Greek Orthodox to come to my meeting.)

forgive us and help us
to serve the ways of reconciliation
according to Thy Will.

Kindle our hearts with the fire of the Holy Spirit.
Give us the spirit of Wisdom and faith, of daring
and of patience, of humility and of firmness, of
love and of repentance, through the prayers of
the most blessed Mother of God and of all the
saints. Amen.

DO YOUR WORK AS FAR AS YOU CAN BUT TAKE CARE NOT TO NEGLECT THE BETTER PART

February 2nd, 1993

(I called the Lord but I could not hear Him - it made me sad. Suddenly the silence was broken by the sound of His step[1] and He spoke to me reproaching me.)

My Spirit is upon you; day and night I have been waiting for you![2] Respect My rules! Why do you hold back our encounters? Now you say, "how long will this last?"[3] when only a few minutes went by, whereas I, I have been waiting for you several days! Until when will I put up with you? You say, your joy lies in being close to Me - wretched you are for good! Puny little creature, do not forget who holds you on your feet; I have treated you kindly and I have been your Support; explain then to Me your absence!

Give the poor and needy another chance! I delight in nothing else on earth than Your Presence!

Choose then to be with Me! I called you to My Heart - I have not called you to administration.

But who will do the work?

---

[1]Figurative.
[2]For three days I did not go to Him in this way.
[3]His absence and His silence.

You have not admitted your sin![1]

Yes, I sinned for not keeping Your rules.

And for not being faithful to Me, say it!

And for not being faithful to You.

Say:

> *I will praise my Lord and*
> *my soul will live for Him alone*
> *and I will serve Him alone, and*
> *my lips will sing for Him alone,*
> *and my heart will*
> *pay attention to Him alone, and*
> *now, my heart will beat for*
> *Him alone.*
>
> *Amen.*[2]

Can the dust praise Me? Can it proclaim praises to Me? No, not unless My Spirit lives inside this dust - without Me you are nothing; the light in your eyes comes from My Light; I will teach you to obey Me for I will level you to the ground - how else will I be seen? I mean to progress you into holiness. ♥ I will crown all My plans with success so do not deny Me from meeting you; do your work as far as you can, but take care not to neglect the better part. Rely on Me to give you support and reinforce you. Pray. We, us?   IΧθΥΣ ⤫⊃

THE VINE I HAD PLANTED IN THE PAST
WILL GIVE ITS FRUIT FOR MY GLORY

February 3rd, 1993

Lord my God, You are known to be quick in generosity for the poor and for the needy. You are known to fill the mouths of the hungry and for those who stretch out their hands to You. You lift the needy giving them a royal place with the elect into

---

[1] The Lord was more severe here than before.
[2] I repeated it after Him.

Your celestial court. You placed the weak into your house. You are known to overthrow kings and kingdoms when they become an obstacle to Your Word. Lord of Tenderness, You look on wretchedness with compassion sending them Wisdom to be their Educator and teach them to walk in Your Presence and enjoy Your favour. Many hound me and oppress me but Your Wisdom taught me that everything is for Your greatest Glory! Unjustifiably men hound me, waiting for me and for the appropriate hour to strike me, Your child, but You are such Joy to me that no matter what men may do to me, I will persevere to proclaim Your Name with Joy. You are such Joy to me that no man, yes, no man can take my eyes away from You. You are immersing perpetually my soul with joy! For You have plunged my soul in a baptism of love, in a baptism of consuming fire leaving my heart ablaze. You have lavished my soul with a vast treasure: that of Your
Sacred Heart.

My child, your endurance will earn you your life - your love and patience will win your place in heaven. My child, My child, let your portion be Me; glorify Me and proclaim to the nations the greatness of My Love. ♥ *Fear no one - I am before you. Raise your eyes and look at Me...[1] I am going to save My people and I will take men from every nation, every race and every language by their sleeve and ask them: "do you want to follow Me?" and they will say: "we want to go with You, since we have now learnt the Truth" and I will bring one after the other back to live in My Heart! I mean to bring peace in each heart. Yes! The vine I had planted in the past will give its fruit for My Glory - I will not be slow nor will I ignore the cries of the faithful.* ♥ *If one man builds My Church while another one pulls it down on whom will the fury of My Father pour out in the Day of Judgement? Hear Me: I have formed you and educated you to revive My Church and bring unity among brothers; I created you, Vassiliki[2] and have called you by your birth-name to be Mine and to come freely into My Presence any time and anywhere you may be[3] - I want you close to Me. O child so favoured by My Father! If I have chosen you to reveal to you the Father and mark you with Our Love and if My Holy Spirit breathed in you reviving you, filling your soul with His Light, transfiguring the Darkness in you into Light, Vassiliki, it is so that the nations see through you My Mercy and My Love. You may ask yourself, "why me? Why has all this happened to me?" I tell you, because of your great misery and your astounding weakness. My Heart, an Abyss of Love, pitied you - it could have been anyone. Do not stand bemused in front of Me! Do you not know your Saviour anymore? Who is there to pity My people if it is not Me? When hordes of nations fall continuously into apostasy and the crown of terror is on every head and when debauchery is ruling their heart, how can I remain silent? Godlessness has spread throughout the world - am I to remain silent? Tell them: happy is the*

---

[1] I raised my eyes and this is what I saw: Christ's Holy Face smiling.
[2] My official birth name.
[3] In this special way.

*heart who will make peace with his brother,[1] for he will be called, child of the
Most High. Happy is the heart who will stop wandering in the night and will
reconcile truly with his brother,[2] not only will he enjoy My favour but truly, I will
reveal to him the Inexhaustible Riches of My Sacred Heart! so that people around
him, astounded by his radiant beauty will say, "truly, God is hidden with him" and
you, daughter, never part from Me. I, the Lord, will shepherd you till the end. ♥
Come.*

THE EARTH WILL SHAKE AND REEL FROM ITS PLACE
UNITY IS UNWELCOMED AS LOVE IS UNWELCOMED

February 18th, 1993

Lord, how long will you allow them[3] to defy You?

When I will speak the next time to them, I will raise a gale!

They scorned Your advices in the ecumenical center (in Mexico city)[4], got up and
left in the middle of the meeting. And as You know, the greatest oppositions in the
World Council of Churches and who did not want my presence there, nor a meeting,
were from my own.

*But I the Victor will bend them double... Look, Vassula-of-My-Passion, have My
Peace - search no one else but Me! Soul-of-My-Passion, go out to the nations and
leave the oppositions to Me - I shall make those that oppose Me get up from their
Seats and bend them double. Trust Me. Go out to the nations and remind
everyone of My Love and that Jesus means Saviour, Redeemer and that the
greatness of My Love for you all surpasses everything... Do not look to your left
nor to your right - remember how My Father seized by your misery gave you His
Peace so that you forward this Peace to everyone. My Father, moved by your
astounding weakness revealed His Face to you and through you to others. My
Holy Spirit enraptured by your nothingness triumphed over you, installing His
Throne in you to rule over your soul, and I filled your heart with the Riches of My
Sacred Heart. Soon, beloved of My Soul, a white linen will cover you and I*

---

[1] Here it means humanity.
[2] Here it means humanity.

[3] The Greek Orthodox ecclesiastics.
[4] All were there. The Greek Orthodox came late, listened for twenty minutes while
I read Jesus' messages of unity, then got up enraged and left.

Myself shall wrap you in My Heart, engulfing you in My Light. ♥ *So My child-of-My-Burning-Passion allow Me to use your little hand for just a while longer.* ♥

Write: I have stepped out of Heaven to reach you, but have you listened to Me? I have stepped out of My Throne to come all the way into your room to court you and remind you that you are heirs to My Kingdom. I have stepped out of My Dwelling Place and have taken the wilderness in search of you - the Master of the heavens has not denied you His Love, never! I have allowed your eyes, creation, to look on a King in His Beauty, to attract you; to honour My Name I have roused the dead to preach to you My Kingdom - where is your response? And you who talk about Unity, do you think empty words will unite you? Who of you is ready to shed all his comforts and follow Me? Tell Me, who of you will be first to end up My Agony and My groans for Unity and Peace before the Hour comes? This Hour that leaves all My angels trembling. Who among you is the soul who will grain the nations with seeds of Love and Peace? Who for My Sake will faithfully follow the Light invoking My Name day and night? Who of you all will be the first to place his feet into My blood-stained Footprints? Are you sincerely seeking Me? See, the days are coming when I am going to come by thunder and Fire but I will find, to My distress, many of you unaware and in deep sleep! I am sending you, creation, messenger after messenger to break through your deafness but I am weary now of your resistance and your apathy. I am ever so weary of your coldness; I am weary of your arrogance and your inflexibility when it comes to assemble for unity - you filled and overflowed now the Cup of Stupor. <u>Intoxicated by your own voice</u> you have opposed My Voice but it shall not be forever - soon you shall fall for you have opposed My Voice by your voice misleading nonsense; naturally My Church is in ruin because of your division. You are not applying My advice nor are you practising My desires for lack of faith, but I will expose your heart to you and to the whole world; I shall expose how secretly you were planning to destroy My Law.[1] The sixth seal is about to be broken[2] and you will all be <u>plunged into darkness</u> and there will be no illumination for the smoke poured up out of the Abyss will be like the smoke from a huge furnace so that the sun and the sky will be darkened by it;[3] and out of My Cup of Justice I will make you resemble snakes; vipers. I will make you crawl on your belly and eat dust[4] in these days of darkness; I will crush you to the ground to remind you that you are not better than vipers... you will suffocate and stifle in your sins; in My anger I will tread you down, trample you in My wrath! See? My four angels are standing anxiously now around My Throne, waiting for My orders; when you will hear peals of thunder and see flashes of lightning know that the Hour of My Justice has

---

[1] Very gravely, Jesus said what follows.
[2] Apocalypse 6:12.
[3] Apocalypse 9:2.
[4] Genesis 3:14.

*come; the earth will shake and like a shooting star will reel from its place,[1]
extirpating mountains and islands out of their places, entire nations will be
annihilated, the sky will disappear like a scroll rolling up[2] as you saw it in your
vision daughter. A great agony will befall on all the citizens, and woe to the
unbeliever! Hear Me: and should men say to you today: "ah, but the Living One
will have Mercy upon us, your prophecy is not from God but from your own spirit"
tell them: although you are reputed to be alive, you are dead; your incredulity
condemns you, because you refused to believe in My time of Mercy and prohibited
My Voice to spread through My mouthpieces to warn and save My creatures - you
shall die too as the bad. When the Hour of Darkness comes, I will show you your
insides; I will turn your soul inside out and when you will see your soul as black
as coal, not only will you experience a distress like never before, but you will beat
your breast with agony saying that your own darkness is far worse than the
darkness surrounding you. As for you,[3] (...) that is how I shall display My Justice
to the nations and all nations will feel My sentence when this Hour comes - I will
make human life scarcer than ever before; then when My wrath will be appeased,
I will set My Throne in each one of you, and together with one voice and one heart
and one language you will praise Me, the Lamb.* ♥

*This is enough for today My Vassula; do not be bitter with your own people, and
do not, soul, trouble your heart either. I shall show you to the world as a sign of
unity; you are contradicted and rejected but you know now why: because unity is
unwelcomed, as Love is unwelcomed in many hearts.* ♥ *Sincerity is missing...
Come, we, us?*

Yes my Lord. **ΙΧθΥΣ** ◁◯▷

MY MERCY IS GREAT,
BUT MY SEVERITY IS AS GREAT

February 19th, 1993

Peace My beloved - are you one with Me?

Make my spirit one with Your Spirit. Only You can do it Lord.

---

[1] Isaiah 13:13.
[2] Apocalypse 6:14.
[3] Concerns me alone.

I am glad that you are conscious of your nothingness and that without Me you can do nothing. ♥ *Lean on Me and I will attract your soul to Me; Love is near you and My Spirit upon you.* ♥ *Allow Me to continue yesterday's Message; hear Me: tell them that mercy and wrath alike belong to Me, who am Mighty to forgive and to pour out wrath. My mercy is great, but My severity is as great.*

(God asked me to write this passage from Ecclesiasticus 16:11,12.)

You see daughter, I will soon reveal My Justice too. ♥ *My Plan has a determined time; My Merciful calls have also a determined time. Once this time of Mercy is over, I will show everyone, good and evil that My severity is as great as My Mercy, that My wrath is as powerful as My forgiveness.* ♥ *All things predicted by Me will pass swiftly now - nothing can be subtracted from them. I have spoken to you of the Apostasy, Apostasy that bound[1] the hands of My best friends, disarming them because of its velocity and its measure; have I not said that cardinals will oppose cardinals and how bishops will go against bishops and that many are on the road to perdition? They have, in their endless battle, weakened My Church. Today this spirit of rebellion thrives inside My Holy Place. Do you recall the vision I had given you of the vipers crawling all over the Holy Sacraments of the altar? Have I not revealed to you how many of them oppose My pope?[2] And how they push him aside?[3] I have already given you a detailed account of the Rebellion inside My Church. My faithful friend, allow Me to stop here - we shall continue later on. Stay near Me and please Me.* ♥

ΙΧθΥΣ ⊂▷

MY WRATH IS AS POWERFUL AS MY FORGIVENESS

February 22, 1993

> "Correct us Yahweh gently, not in Your anger, or You will reduce us to nothing."
>
> Jr 10:24

Vassula, messenger follows close on messenger, to tell the world to repent. I am manifesting Myself like never before to bring everyone from far away back to Me

---

[1] It means they were helpless.
[2] Pope John-Paul II.
[3] Previous message.

and follow My Commandments. At any moment this little flame flickering inside this generation would die down if I do not intervene; even to this day they refuse to hear and believe. The greater they think they are the less they are in My Eyes, how could they find favour with Me when they obstruct My Holy Spirit? What I hear from them is: "Who has authority over me?" "I am self-sufficient." My compassion is great but My severity is as great. ♥ My wrath is as powerful as My forgiveness. My temples[1] have now a common ground with traders; they have exchanged My Holiness for a tribute to Satan! I am speaking of those who apostatised and have allowed a Lie to pass their lips and now they intend to compel everyone to be branded with that Lie and I am tired of bearing them. In My House once, integrity lived there since My Law was their daily bread, but look at what My House has become now - a desolation, a haunt for the lizard and the spider! Ah... but I will undo all this. My Heart is broken within Me, My child, and My angels dread and tremble for the Hour I reserved to break out when My orders will be given. I cannot endure any more to see your Holy Mother's Tears shed over and over again every time My Son is recrucified; your generation's sins are leading My Son to Calvary every moment.

Together in one voice the world is blaspheming My Holy Spirit and all the powers of heaven. Daily, the world is provoking Me: "Look! Look what has become of the great Lord's House?" they say, while tearing It down and dissembling then. My Soul cannot bear any longer the groans of My Son being recrucified, although both My Son and your Holy Mother muffle as best they could their pain. My Ears hear everything; My Ears and My Eyes are not human and nothing escapes Me. Since it is your generation that makes the choice, not I,[2] the Rebellion in My House will bring down on you My wrath and the deepest Darkness is wrought on earth soon; it is not My choice but yours. I had chosen to lift you from your graves with Mercy and Love, Compassion and Peace, but look how so many of you are unmoved to My offer, nothing can touch you any longer.

My Patience you have exhausted and you, daughter, be My Echo. Hard as they may harass you, I shall not allow them to overcome you. On the contrary, you will be like a sword when you will pronounce My words; remind them again that I take pleasure, not in the death of a wicked and rebellious man but in the turning back of a wicked and rebellious man who changes his ways to win life. This earth that you know 'will vanish soon!'[3] I have decided to hasten My Plan because of the great sins your generation conceives. All will vanish, all will wear out like a garment.[4] This will be My way of destroying the defilement of sin, and you will

---

[1] I understood: souls
[2] That is: instead of choosing God's Peace we choose to pass into the new era by God's Chastisement.
[3] Heb. 1:11
[4] Ap. 21:1 and 4

realize that from the beginning you were My sacred temples and that My Spirit was living in you. Ah! for this Baptism by Fire!! Pray and fast in these last days. I Am is near you. ♥

PUBLISHER AND DISTRIBUTOR

United Kingdom

J.M.J. Publications (Chris Lynch)
P.O. Box 385
Belfast, Northern Ireland
BT9 6RQ
Fax: (0232) 381596

NATIONAL DISTRIBUTORS

United States

John Lynch
319 North Virginia Ave
North Massapequa, N.Y.
U.S.A. 11758
Tel: (516) 293-9635

Canada

Caravan Agencies Ltd
6 Dumbarton Blvd.
Winnipeg, Manitoba
Canada R3P 2C4
Tel/Fax: (204) 895-8878

Australia

Carley LeGrand
Medjugorje Centre for Peace
91 Auburn Road
Auburn, Victoria
Australia 3123
Tel: (03) 882-9822
Fax: (03) 882-9675

South Africa

Winnie Williams
Friends of Medjugorje
P.O. Box 32817
Braamfontein 2017
Johannesburg, South Africa
Tel: (011) 640-6583
Fax: (011) 339-7185

TITLES AVAILABLE - TRUE LIFE IN GOD

Volume I (Notebooks 1-31)

Guardian angel Daniel, prepares Vassula to meet Jesus. Jesus teaches Vassula love of God, the scriptures; describes His passion; His love of 'daughter' Russia and its resurrection; the Great Apostasy. He links Garabandal to Fatima; His desire for unity of the Churches. *(UK£8 IR£9 CND$17 US$14)*

Volume II (Notebooks 32-58)

Jesus teaches that God is alive and very near, desiring a return to love, Adoration, sharing His Passion, consoling Him; return of Jesus. He teaches about the state of the Church, His shepherds; the renewal of His vineyards; Devotion to the Two Sacred Hearts of Jesus and Mary; expands on the ten commandments and Beatitudes; Apocalypse 12. The rebellion in the Church and the Great Apostasy; the suffering of His Peter; the minature judgement; unrolling of the 'scrolls.' Many prayers, of consecration, of adoration, of consolation, praise etc... to Father, Son and Holy Spirit. *(UK£8 IR£9 Cdn$17 US$14)*

Prayers of Jesus and Vassula

A beautiful assortment of prayers, some given by Jesus, others by Vassula, inspired by the Holy Spirit. A section on the Devotion to the Two Hearts; Daily Prayers and quotations of Jesus' teaching how to pray. *(UK£3.75 IR£4.50 Cdn$7 US$5.50)*

Vassula of the Sacred Heart's Passion by Michael O'Carroll C.S.Sp.

A 220 page book giving an outline of Vassula's life, her charism and analysis of Jesus' messages in the light of the teaching of the Church. Also a message to cardinals, bishops and priests of 'The Rebel' with a warning not to listen or follow the teaching of anyone except the Holy Father, John Paul II. (17 March 1993) *(UK£5.50 IR£6 Cdn$10 US$8.50)*

See Distributors list at end of this book. Discounts available for bookstores.

Mailing: *(Please add to order)*

UK/Ireland : 1 Book £2   2 Books £3
USA   : 1 Book $3.50 2 Books $4.50